# AMISH

## THE ART OF THE QUILT

Text

# Robert Hughes

Plate Commentary

# Julie Silber

# FOREWORD

A couple of years ago, I was leading a tour through the Esprit quilt collection with a group of

women, one of whom had a small boy about six. The mother was busy translating some of my

more "grown-up" comments about the quilts to her son, who was obviously enjoying himself

tremendously. When we turned a corner and came upon one particularly colorful quilt, the

little boy whooped, "Oh, Mommy, I *love* this one," rushed right over to the quilt and kissed it!

While we must unfortunately discourage such physical displays of enthusiasm, we warmly

invite you to enjoy along with us the many pleasures of having what is perhaps the world's

finest collection of antique Amish quilts.

The Esprit quilt collection was always meant to be shared. From its beginnings in 1971,

when quilts first went up on the walls of the company's San Francisco headquarters, the

collection was designed to be seen. It has been from the start extraordinarily accessible to

the public. With a call ahead, anyone who wishes can visit Esprit's offices at 900 Minnesota

Street on weekdays during regular business hours. We make the collection available in a

number of other ways. Over the years, pieces from it have been included in exhibitions and

publications worldwide. In 1990, we organized a major exhibition of the Esprit collection

with The Fine Arts Museums of San Francisco. Finally, this volume, published internationally,

fulfills our longtime dream of presenting these superb quilts in the finest possible edition.

We are delighted that in all these ways many thousands of people can share in the enjoyment

of our quilt collection.

Esprit has an inclusive and consistent aesthetic, of which the quilts are a part. This aesthetic is maintained because Doug Tompkins oversees every aspect of the company's design. Underlying principles of practicality and good design guide Doug's unrelenting attention to detail in every aspect of the business. From the products to the architecture, from the packaging to the park beside the offices, from the handmade desks to the presentation of the food in the café, this is a singular vision: one person's fine eye, set of beliefs, regard for craftsmanship and quality—one person's sensibilities.

As soon as you walk into the company's headquarters, something happens to you. The quilts combine with the handmade furniture and exposed structural elements of the building to give a feeling of visual pleasure and warmth.

The interior of the century-old brick building is simple and undecorated. The walls are functional and proportioned. The interior is harmonized, with few surfaces. It is basically a beige interior with blue doors. And quilts. Luminous objects in a neutral space.

A dramatic quilt is hung inside the entry, inviting visitors to wander through the collection of nearly two hundred pieces. The quilts are displayed all through the 110,000-square-foot building, in both private offices and public spaces on brick, wood, concrete or plasterboard walls. The size and shape of the interior nonbearing walls were specifically designed to frame the quilts in white. In keeping with Doug's view of the quilts as "painterly," the quilts are stretched rather taut (without straining the fibers) to emphasize their hard edge, underplaying

T

the softness and the fragility of the materials. Long, dramatic sight lines give visitors a choice of views: at a distance, to enjoy various combinations of quilts or the graphic impact of one entire quilt; up close, to appreciate the details and craft of each piece more intimately. Variations on fundamental design elements make for quiet surprises as well as a pleasing continuity in the quilts.

Although quilts from North America's many Amish communities are represented, the Esprit collection does not pretend to be comprehensive nor representative of all Amish quilts. Doug has a distinct preference, indeed a passion, for the quilts made by the Amish women of Lancaster County, Pennsylvania, between 1870 and 1950. Their stunning quilts dominate the collection at Esprit and are the quilts represented in this volume.

What is it about these Lancaster Amish quilts that is so compelling? For Doug, it is primarily a visual matter. To him, Lancaster quilts are masterpieces of design. The pure geometric forms and unexpected, sumptuous color combinations come together in works of extraordinary power and vitality. With their austere formats and plain cloth, Lancaster quilts are, to Doug, "a first statement of design principles—simple and absolute." I have a different approach: quilts are indeed beautiful objects, and they are more. They embody many levels of meaning. I see them as fabric "documents," holding within them the lives of the women who made them and the people who lived with them. So, for me, the Esprit collection is Amish quilts and Amish people; it is both a body of magnificent

8  design and a window into the fascinating culture and the times that produced it.

When I became the collection's first curator in 1983, Doug and I began integrating our different perspectives. His point of view is realized in the graphic presentation of the collection, mine in verbal interpretations of the objects. Doug designs exhibitions of our quilts, both in and out of our building, as well as all our quilt publications, including this book. He chooses to visually isolate the quilts, separating them from their original context and their past network of associations. By introducing them in a new environment, he feels that the timelessness and universality of their art come through. For me, the visual experience of these quilts has been tremendously enriched by getting to know about the culture that produced them. So I use words to bring to the quilts what I have learned about the Amish. In this book, I have written commentaries on each quilt, incorporating bits of information on the social context in which the quilts were made and used. I also do so when I lead tours of the collection at company headquarters, organize informal seminars for Esprit employees and lecture around the country. In the interplay of graphics and interpretation, Doug and I have found a satisfying, mutually enriching way to wed our points of view.

At Esprit, the quilt collection is integral. For those of us who work here, the quilts are part of our lives every day; customers and other clients enjoy them whenever they come. People who might never visit a gallery or museum are informally exposed to them. In addition, people from all over the world come to Esprit specifically to enjoy a unique corporate art collection.

We invite you to take some time with these marvelous pieces. They can be enjoyed on

many levels and in many ways. Look at them, study them each alone and in relation to the others. Notice how even very similar quilts evoke different feelings. Imagine the women who made them, the people who lived with them, the times and places in which they were used. Quilts were made with love and were meant to be shared. Please enjoy them now with us.

Julie Silber

# THE ART OF THE QUILT

By

Robert Hughes

To make a quilt you take three pieces of cloth—top, bottom and filling in between—and sew them together to make a kind of padded blanket. A simple idea that leads to strange and exalted complications, takes thousands of woman-hours and has much to say about American history.

This is a particularly, if not uniquely, American form, an art based on strict modular arrangements, intricate geometry, luscious colors—and salvage, not-wasting, "making do."

The quilt is where the desire for beauty and the moral scorn for extravagance used to intersect. And being made by women from colored cloth, rather than by men out of "nobler" stuff—like colored muds and chemicals smeared on canvas—it has long been regarded as a somewhat minor art form.

This archaic prejudice is not likely to survive a thoughtful tour of the collection that Doug Tompkins and Julie Silber have assembled for Esprit. The Esprit collection is not meant to be a historical survey of American quiltmaking as a whole. Rather, it concentrates on quilts made by one religious group, the Amish, and its particular field is the work of Pennsylvania Amish quilt-makers. (There are Amish in twenty states of the United States, but most of them live in the East in Pennsylvania and in the Midwestern states of Indiana and Ohio.) To traverse this collection with open eyes is to realize that the quilt, especially the pieced Amish quilt, and more especially still the work of Amish quiltmakers in Lancaster County, Pennsylvania, between about 1870 and 1950, was one of the finest aesthetic forms in America.

It was also a curiously prophetic form, even though the prophecy went without honor for so long. For where have we seen images something like these before? In much later, "professional" (as opposed to "folk") art: in the explicit geometries of the sixties and seventies, the stripes and targets of Noland, the concentric squares of early Stella, in Sol Lewitt's grids and the blocks of muted, saturated color deployed by Brice Marden; in the whole emphasis on seriality, repetition and exalted emotional silence that was the mark of a certain phase of American modernism. Just as the dazzle of op art is prefigured—though with more subtlety than anything Vasarely or Anuszkiewicz could produce in the sixties—in Sunshine and Shadow quilts like plates 28 and 30, so the austerity of the centered Diamond in the Square and Center Square designs such as plates 9 and 1 may be allowed to evoke the words of the patron saint of American minimalism, Ad Reinhardt: "The creative process is always an academic routine and sacred procedure. Everything is prescribed and proscribed. Only in this way is there no grasping or clinging to anything. Only a standard form can be imageless, only a stereotyped image can be formless, only a formulaized [*sic*] art can be formulaless."

Puritan in its historical origins yet permeated by myths of its own Paradisiacal excess, American culture has always oscillated between bone and breast, the minimal and the maximal. These quilts could almost be seen as an unconscious effort to harmonize the two: a warm, soft, swaddling minimalism. But seen out of their original context of use, hanging on a wall, they make it very plain how absurd the once jealously guarded hierarchical distinctions between "folk" and "high" art can be. These aesthetically radiant objects have survived their forced transition from folkishness to the culture of the museum. They have done so, in part at least, because they are just a tad more aloof than most of the things that folk cultures produce.

Folk art, like vernacular speech, may be whimsical. It is never inflated. It wants to be understood by everyone who sees it, and so it tends toward concision and practicality. It is filled with the marks of real social life—clues to hopes, values and aspirations that you feel you can read with trust because they have not been given rhetorical form. The period 1870–1930, during which most of the Amish quilts in this collection were made, was the last in which America had a widespread, vital and self-sufficient pattern of folk culture that expressed itself in the visual arts.

But this tradition only came to be valued when it was almost gone. Folk art went because folk went. Part of America, old America, the primitive republic of independence and self-help, was disappearing, and its records had to be kept. Its forms would very soon be diluted and destroyed—and then "revived" as tourist emblems or nostalgic images—by the inexorable pressures of the late nineteenth and early twentieth century.

Mass production meant buying things ready-made, first from peddlers and then at stores, instead of making them oneself. Isolated farms and whole hamlets found themselves drawn into the mainstream by traveling salesmen, cars, phones, radio and the impact of the common imagery of the movies. Clans could no longer hold together; the pull of the larger community was too great.

By the fifties there was a whole popular imagery of folk stubbornness and folk displacement, running from the cult of Grandma Moses at one end of the scale to Ma and Pa Kettle and the Beverly Hillbillies at the other. Travel brought tourists, who wanted the "typical" and the "quaint," pressing folk art to become culturally self-conscious.

Today, almost all "folk art" in America is meant to be bought by people from outside the community in which it is made. This is also true of the Amish, who—owing to their apartness, their binding sense of themselves as a group of the Elect whose survival depended entirely on not having much truck with the "English" culture that surrounded them—nevertheless held out longer than most.

## II

Quiltmaking was a women's art form. Not just something that women as well as men did, like sculpture or easel painting; but something mainly, if not quite only, done by women. Quilts made by American men do exist, but they were almost always made under special conditions—convalescence, retirement, imprisonment or service on shipboard. All these were forms of confinement, an exception for men but something much closer to normality for women. Some Amish men did "try their hand" at cutting and piecing quilts, but only when age or disability kept them from farming. They never seem to have designed them.

But virtually all Amish women were quiltmakers. Piecing (the assembly, to a design, of the patchwork surface of the top layer) and quilting (the assembly of the layers with tens of thousands of running stitches through the fabric, the lines of stitching laid out in the strictest order and pattern as a counterpoint to the pieced design) were always done by women—the piecing and the design of the quilting pattern by the individual housewife, the finishing often by women in groups, gathered for the pleasures and mutual support of the "quilting bee." By the 1880s, American women were struggling to make their professional mark on wider aesthetic fields. There were female students in most art academies, from Thomas Eakins' classes in Philadelphia to the ateliers of Paris—Cormon's, Colarossi's, Gerome's. Not one of them, with the single exception of Mary Cassatt, was going to have more than a peripheral effect on the culture of her time. There is no simple answer as to why this should have been so.

The idea that it was entirely due to hostile male domination of the art world is as naive and misleading as the patriarchal notion that women suffered from a communal, gender-determined lack of talent, a proclivity to "taste" but not "genius." Most art made by women, like most art made by men, is mediocre; inside that framework, the fact that some painting was made by a woman no more places it in a special aesthetic category than the circumstance that it was made by a left-hander. Not until long after Georgia O'Keeffe's first one-woman show at the 291 Gallery in 1917 would that begin to change.

In folk art, which was produced and used outside the formal structures of the American "art world" and the society it was trying to address in New York, Boston and Chicago, the position of women was quite different. Women had always been accepted as primary creators of folk art. Most of the finest works of art made by women in the late nineteenth century came from people who had no ideas at all about a career as professional artists— including the wives and daughters of Amish farmers.

The trouble was that folk art, until about fifty years ago, was not generally seen as art, or not as art that really "mattered."

Not until the Abby Aldrich Rockefeller Folk Art Collection became the nucleus of a special area of study within the then new Museum of Modern Art (most of it was later transferred to Williamsburg, Virginia) did the importance of folk art to American history become recognized. Folk art tells us a host of things about the common life of its society that are not raised by "professional" art, whether made by traditionalist or radical. It is not about superfluity or excess; its purpose is not to give the official version. There is, of course, no such thing as avant-garde folk art, because small rural communities are intrinsically conservative and could not care less about myths of the cultural future. "The old is the best, and the new is of the devil."

In looking at such things we have to drop the snootiness that goes with looking at the artifacts of a "simpler" way of life than ours, because the life of rural communities is not simple and never was. By the same token it is a good idea to think twice about the figure of the folk artist as "humble," "anonymous," craftsman or craftswoman. This, like the noble savage, is a figment of the sophisticated. One sees why as soon as one asks, Anonymous to whom? Things become "anonymous" when they leave home and drift into the market, because they lose their domestic history and cease to be triggers of memory—"That was the quilt Grandmother Fischer made for Maria when she was five." But they were not "anonymous" when they were made. On the contrary: these quilts were the intense and focused expression not of some generalized idea of women as a class, but of individual people making them for their families and proud of their skills. Everyone who saw them knew who made them. To treat such things as "anonymous" merely because they are not signed is implicitly to collapse the social space around them.

Just as we know that our culture can neither surpass nor even adequately mimic the unfussed refinement of good Shaker furniture—a refinement that rises from practical economy disciplined by the literal belief that God, in Mies van der Rohe's phrase, is in the details—so we recognize in a fine Amish quilt a spareness of design just pulled back from dogmatic rigor by its inventive quirks, a magnificent sobriety of color, a balanced amplitude of conception, a truly human sense of scale. Since these are not, on the whole, the common traits of American art in the late 1980s, they make the quilts reproduced on the pages that follow seem like emissaries from a vanished world.

It is not the world of our lost parents or great-grandparents, either. How could it be? We did not know that world, even vicariously. Few of us, if any, have Amish sitting gravely in our family trees. The Amish are and always have been a small and conservative group, willing themselves apart from the teeming, melding population of the American mainstream and careful to maintain their polite but rigorous distance from the values of urban-industrial America. They enormously outnumber the Shakers—there are perhaps one hundred thousand Amish distributed across twenty states of the United States and one Canadian province, three-quarters of whom live in Pennsylvania, Indiana and Ohio; whereas a few years ago, there were no more than a dozen practicing Shakers, all women between fifty and eighty years of age. Nevertheless, most Americans, if they have heard about the Amish, have only a vague picture of them. It is a Wyeth-tinted time warp, amplified maybe by Peter Weir's film *Witness,* in which hirsute patriarchs in baggy trousers drive their buggies while Fords zip past on the near but infinitely distant freeway. Few non-Amish have much exposure to Amish ways, past or present.

So one thinks of them as "folk," quaint in their plainness and otherness and, like all "folk," given to producing a recognizable cultural secretion known as "folk art." But if "folk art" means images that high taste can condescend to in the very act of savoring them, then Lancaster quilts are not folk art—or not of that kind. They radiate a fierce stylistic distinction, a forthright economy of means, a syntax that is governed by strict traditions and yet looks inescapably modern. They are a "high" enclave within the general taste even of Amish quiltmaking.

The broad differences between Pennsylvania Amish quilts in Lancaster County and those from Amish communities in Midwestern states (Ohio and Indiana) can be briefly put. Lancaster quilts have large, geometrical color-fields, unlike the busier Midwestern Amish patchwork patterns. They use deep, saturated colors, but not black, a great favorite in the American heartland. They have their own peculiar designs, like the Diamond in the Square, whereas Midwestern Amish quilts use traditional American designs like Baskets and Baby's Blocks. Their favorite format is a central medallion, as against the Midwestern preference for repeated, all-over blocks. Their quilting is incomparably more elaborate than that of the Midwestern Amish, and done in contrasting thread. They tend to be made of fine wool, not cotton.

And they have no depictive imagery at all; they are not covered with the emblems of day-to-day life one finds on some other

American quilts—animals and people and tools and trees and locomotives. You cannot look at them and think, How cute. Perhaps you cannot help thinking, How modern. But that is an illusion: the truth is that Amish quilts embody the reductionism, the search for fundamentals, that modernism wanted to find in more "primitive" cultures, but they are no more modern than a Fang mask is cubist. In fact, they come from a culture to which modernism is anathema.

### III

The Amish are a religious offshoot of the Anabaptists, a radical Protestant sect that rose in the sixteenth century in rebellion against the "impure," "worldly" Roman Catholic Church, advocating a return to the pacifism and communism preached in the Sermon on the Mount and a complete separation between church and state. A minority of extremist Anabaptists, who believed that the millennium was at hand and that the rule of the Elect would be preceded by a catastrophic battle between Good and Evil, provoked a peasants' uprising against both Catholic and Lutheran authority, led by a demented charismatic named Jan of Munster, who hoped to establish the Kingdom of God on earth; he and most of his followers were slaughtered. But the saner majority of Anabaptists, from whom all Amish communities in the United States are descended, wished only to have freedom of their own religion. Some fled *en groupe* to Zurich and settled as mountain farmers in the Bernese Oberland, renaming themselves the Swiss Brethren. Others went to the Netherlands and called themselves Mennonites, after their pastor Menno Simons (1496–1561). The Swiss Brethren continued to be persecuted for another two centuries, and in the process they split: a new sect, led by the pastor Jakob Ammann, took the name of Amish. Before long, there were Amish communities from Bern, through Alsace, to the Rhenish Palatinate: small, agrarian, "primitive," literal-minded in their approach to Scripture and fiercely conservative.

Persecution forced them to start moving out of Bern and the Palatinate; like other groups, including the Mennonites, they saw America as the new blank slate on which ideal social inscriptions could be written by the Elect. The first Amish migration came to Pennsylvania in 1737 and was followed by groups in the 1740s and 1750s; it was complete by 1754. A second wave (mostly from Alsace) came between 1815 and 1860.

No tradition of quiltmaking, it seems, came with them. There are no known Amish quilts that can be dated earlier than one from 1849, and the next datable one was made sometime around 1860. The aesthetic maturity of their quilts begins well after they were settled as an American minority, and they learned the techniques from other settled Americans, probably their Mennonite neighbors, the (relatively) liberal Pennsylvania Germans who were known as the "Gay Dutch." This is no surprise, since although patchwork quilting was certainly done in England and Scotland as early as the seventeenth century, it was never a major form of Dutch or German folk art—not, certainly, to the extent that it would become one in America.

The conventional reason given for the growth of the American quilt used to be simple: thrift. But that is too simple. Thrift alone does not produce an art form, or account for all the kinds of social use represented by the quilt. The aesthetic motive was always foremost in quilting. Yet it is true that one difference between early and late American quilts was supply. The "explosion" in quilting after the mid-nineteenth century could not have happened without the wide availability of cheap cotton fabrics, which gave the "quilt aesthetic" its everyday and necessary material. A century earlier, the colonies had no way of producing a variety of textiles. Small mills were set up during the Revolution —England's sea embargo made them necessary—and the first American textile machines were installed in Rhode Island by Samuel Slater in 1793. But despite these late and primitive beginnings, most cloth (and, of course, all luxury fabrics) still would have had to be imported even if fashion had not attached its value to the exotic and rare. Woolens and plain cottons came from Manchester, the silks from China, the delicate and much-prized printed calicoes from India. On the other side of the Atlantic, where whole cloth and woven blankets were easy and cheap to buy, the impulse to save every scrap of cloth and reuse it was not so strong. But in America, even on its prosperous Eastern shore, every household worthy of the name had its scrap bag: in 1651 the inventory of a Boston shopkeeper named Henry Landis lists such fabrics as "black Turky tamet, linsie woolsey, broadcloth, tamy cheny, adretto, herico Italiano, sad hair coloured Italiano, say, red satinesco tufted Holland, broad dowlas, white calico," and offcuts of these imports would be duly bundled under hun-

dreds of Boston sewing tables, the scrap stuff of quilts to come. Printed fabrics—imported Indian chintzes and the now exceptionally rare copper-printed cottons made in Benjamin Franklin's day (and sometimes at his urging) by such local firms as John Hewson's in Philadelphia—were also thriftily saved. Inserted into the quilt's larger matrix of common cloth, these fabrics produced a memory of elaboration at very little cost. And the plainer materials like homespun and store-bought cotton, once pieced together into the often amazingly intricate designs that abounded in American "secular" quilts of the late eighteenth and nineteenth centuries, and enhanced with every kind of embroidery and appliqué-work, could show a lovely balance between the technically sumptuous and the naively pictorial, as in the famous Sarah Furman Warner quilt, circa 1800, in the Henry Ford Museum in Dearborn, Michigan.

Plain cloth, however, was the only stuff of Amish quilts. The

Amish never use prints, patterns or scraps with any kind of pre-existing internal design. Hence the very thing that gives so many American quilts their period charm and their historical eloquence —namely, their depictive element—is lacking in Amish work. The Amish, for instance, rarely went in for that pervasive folk-art form, the so-called Friendship or Album quilt, belonging to the years of westward migration after 1840. Families and some-times whole communities would join together to design, piece and assemble a quilt as a parting gift for a woman about to embark on the long, hard, perilous journey west. Each person would make her or his patch, carrying a signature, a line from the popular poetry of the day, a motto, a design or a biblical text. The Friendship quilt, assembled by so many hands, translated social warmth directly into physical warmth and went along in the wagon as a treasured symbol of "belonging" that could mitigate, at least in memory, the lonely, grinding harshness of frontier life. But only a minority of the Amish—some "second-comers" to Indiana, Oklahoma and Kansas—were frontier folk, real sod-busters. Most Amish settlers were prosperous farmers in the second and third waves of migration, and they tended to move as a community. Such people were less likely to need albums to remind them of a lost security, and their quilts tend not to be explicit records of social sentiment. Nevertheless, Friendship quilts (whose blocks would be initialed by the contributors, though never embellished with mottoes and inscriptions) were not unknown among the Amish. But they did not go in for the didactic messages, the recording of their responses to large social issues like the temperance movement that bore on the lives of American women and are emblazoned on hundreds of quilts made outside the confines of Amish society.

## IV

Why was this so? Students of Amish ways have never been able to discover anything like a "theory" of quiltmaking held by the Amish themselves. The Amish talk about quiltmaking as a purely practical matter: they do it to keep warm. This would seem to fly in the face of reason, since there are, to put it mildly, much easier ways to obtain a blanket than by patiently expending hundreds or thousands of hours on piecing, patching, assembly and quilting. What we have here is an activity that is part practical, part aesthetic and part ritualistic, a social binder. It is not "pure" creativity, but neither is it "pure" use. Amish quilts adhere to a strict repertoire of patterns but have no religious iconography in the real sense of the word: though critics in the wake of Thomas Hess and Harold Rosenberg used to imagine that Barnett Newman's vertical "zip" could mean anything from Adam to Yahweh himself, the Amish are more modest about the meanings of their art. Quiltmaking falls under the general rubric of what the Amish call the *Ordnung* (pronounced "artning"), an oral tradition of religious rules governing social customs, moral life and work that has descended—branching and changing as it went, throughout the various Amish subgroups—from the sixteenth century. It directs the Amish toward the cardinal virtues of their social ethic: humility and non-resistance, simplicity and practicality. Many details of daily life are covered in the *Ordnung*, from the length of beards or skirts to bans on harness ornament, "showy" linoleum and radios. Apparently, though, the *Ordnung* says nothing specific about quilts as such, or about their design.

Nevertheless, it has clearly affected both, because the *Ordnung* is an instrument of intense cultural as well as moral conservatism. There was a schism among the Amish in Pennsylvania around

1942, over the question of whether houses could have projecting eaves at their gable ends. The *Ordnung* forbade such eaves as showy and "worldly." A family of the Old Order, or Yoder, Amish persuasion had bought a farmhouse from a non-Amish family. They did not want to saw off its eaves. The elders insisted they should. From this doctrinal wrangle (in the course of which one dissenting Amishman expressed his solidarity with the heretics by building a doghouse with gable eaves sticking out, a radical gesture if ever there was one) a new subgroup, the Zook Amish, was born. However, the only difference that an outsider could detect between Zooks and Yoders was that one had eaves on their houses and the other did not. (Hostetler, *Amish Society*, 238–39.) Societies like this are not, if one may so frame the point, rich seedbeds for stylistic innovation. And so the designs of Lancaster Amish quilts in particular—allowing for certain variations from family to family, district to district—tend toward a "conservative" central-medallion form, whether Square, Bars or Diamond. (There are a few Lancaster County Amish quilts in the form of a star, and the Esprit collection contains one magnificent example, a Lancaster Lone Star from 1920, plate 82.) Likewise, the cultural pressure of the *Ordnung* favors sober colors as emblems, not quite metaphors, of moral states. Lancaster Amish quilts have a rich palette of saturated colors, which suggests both gravity and fullness and suits a culture that puts a tremendous premium on stable order and material adequacy. White and yellow are not used, though when the Amish moved west into America, to Iowa, Kansas and Nebraska, they began to put the brighter colors— some groups using oranges and yellows, others preferring white— into their designs. In the classic days of Amish quiltmaking, all designs were made from the kind of cloth used for dresses and shirts. Lancaster County Amish quiltmakers, in particular, would buy this cloth by the yard for their designs, just as an artist buys the paint he or she needs: they did not wait until suitable scraps accumulated. Under the black coats and capes Amish men and women wear in public, these shirts and dresses could be bright. But the color of the quilts mirrored the sumptuary restrictions placed on the color of clothes, and the *Ordnung* could be quite specific about that, if one can judge from one of its rare printed forms, set out in a tract by the Amish of Pike County, Ohio, in 1950: "No ornamental, bright, showy, form-fitting, immodest or silk-like clothing of any kind. Colors such as bright red, orange, yellow or pink not allowed." (Ibid., 59.) But if scarlet might suggest the Whore of Babylon to one group of Amish in Ohio, it did not to others elsewhere: "turkey red," that deep singing red between carmine and burgundy that recurs in Lancaster quilts, was a favorite throughout Pennsylvania.

And so, Amish quilts in general are not conceived as collages in cloth, full of micro-images snipped from the flux of daily life. They are distanced, august and austerely geometrical. The Amish central medallion, a Center Square or Diamond, was opposed to the repeated-block design common among other American quilts of the period. It confirms, one might say, a "conservative" liking for figure-ground relations as against an "advanced" preference for all-overness. The almost liturgical grandeur of a design like that in plate 17, a 1930s Diamond quilt from Lancaster County, seems to look back to the architectural inlays of the Tuscan quattrocento, whereas the repeated-motif blocks of popular non-Amish quilts might appear, if you care to stretch a point, to predict Andy Warhol and his rows of soup cans. Even when the Amish were influenced by repeated-block designs, as in plate 63, a Fourpatch (Variation) pattern quilt, a nostalgia for their medallion would often persist: the bright red "cross" centers the whole design and deprives it of its all-overness.

The dislike of "worldliness"—for which read "showiness"—means that the elaborate detailing of other American quilts is repressed in Amish work. One can readily see why: it would look as though the maker had spent too much time on the quilt, at the expense of her other social and domestic duties; it could suggest idleness or, worse, a certain frivolity, both repugnant to the *Ordnung*. The stricter the group, the more common the process of "saving" will tend to be: thus Old Order or "Nebraska" Amish quilts are apt to incorporate more worn, recycled material than those of less conservative groups, which used new cloth, scraps of bolts rather than scraps of clothing. Likewise, Midwest Amish work seems, in general, to be less elaborately (though no less finely) quilted than that of other Amish communities and has fewer large plain areas to show off the stitching patterns. But the skill of Amish needleworkers is always on parade in the quilting in those precise, unwavering curves, sometimes though not always drawn out with standard templates, through which the lines of running stitch describe the stylized forms of swag, leaf, rose petal, basket, urn and spray, the figurative counterpoint to the abstract grandeur of the large color design.

In any case no custom, however strict, is going to suppress an artist's inventive powers. The Amish did not make crazy quilts for some decades after the general vogue for them in America peaked, but when they did, as in plate 81, they could give the form an entrancing visual gravity—the interlocks of form and color in the sixteen square "windows" being held and restrained, but not overwhelmed, by the grid of bars whose color shifts gently from pale lilac to off-white. In their complexity, visual intensity and quality of craftsmanship, such works simply dispel the idea that folk art is innocent social birdsong. They are as much a part of the story of high aesthetic effort in America as any painting or sculpture. They deserve our attention and abundantly repay it.

My thanks go to Julie Silber for her generous sharing of her scholarly information with a neophyte, and to Eve Granick, Jonathan Holstein and Pat Ferrero for taking the time to read and correct the first draft of this essay.

# PLATES

Plate Commentary

Julie Silber

# C e n t e r   S q u a r e

*Unknown Amish quiltmaker, American, Lancaster County, Pennsylvania, Circa 1890, Pieced wools,  78 x 79 inches, 585.128*

Lancaster Amish quilts are characteristically made from a very few pieces—large geometric fields of solid-colored fabrics.
None is as minimal as the Center Square, the purest of all their designs. The simple box and surrounding borders are showplaces for their elegant,
masterly quilting, which here covers the surface of the quilt.

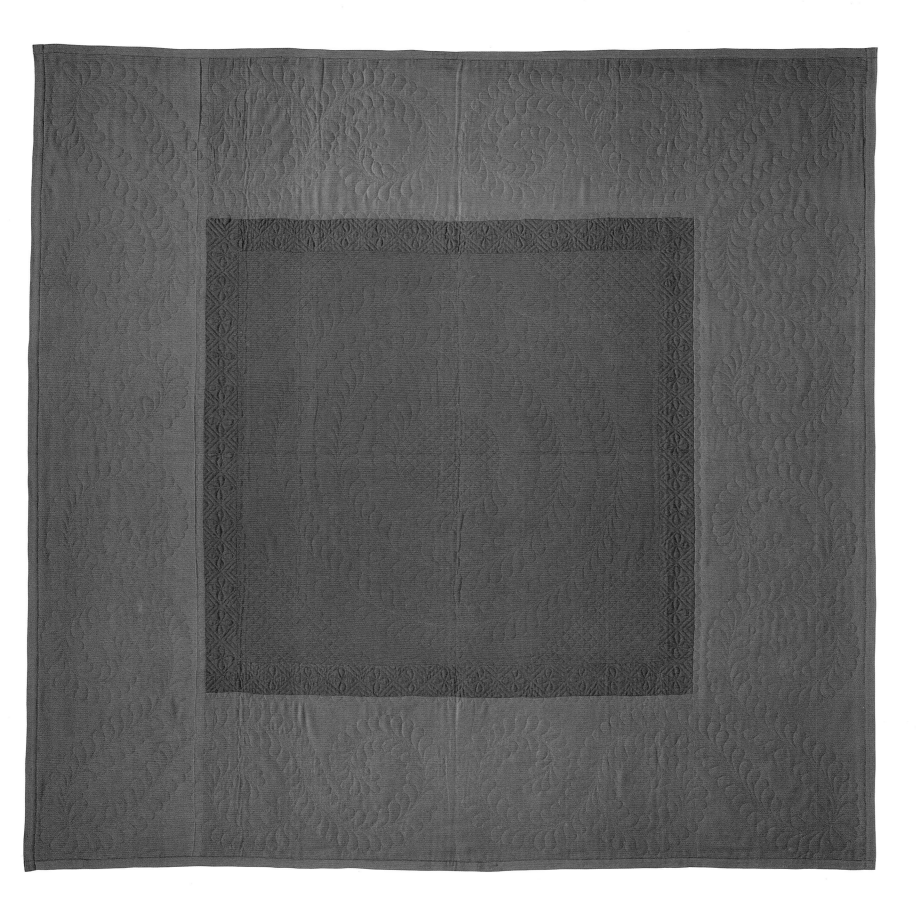

## C e n t e r   S q u a r e

*Unknown Amish quiltmaker, American, Lancaster County, Pennsylvania, Circa 1890, Pieced wools, 78 x 78 inches, 585.297*

Very few early examples of Lancaster Amish quilts remain, so it is difficult to be certain of how design developed. It is likely, however, that the Center Square represents an early stage in Lancaster Amish quilt design, preceded by the whole-cloth (unpieced, but fully quilted) type, and followed by the Diamond in the Square. Few Center Square quilts were made after the nineteenth century.

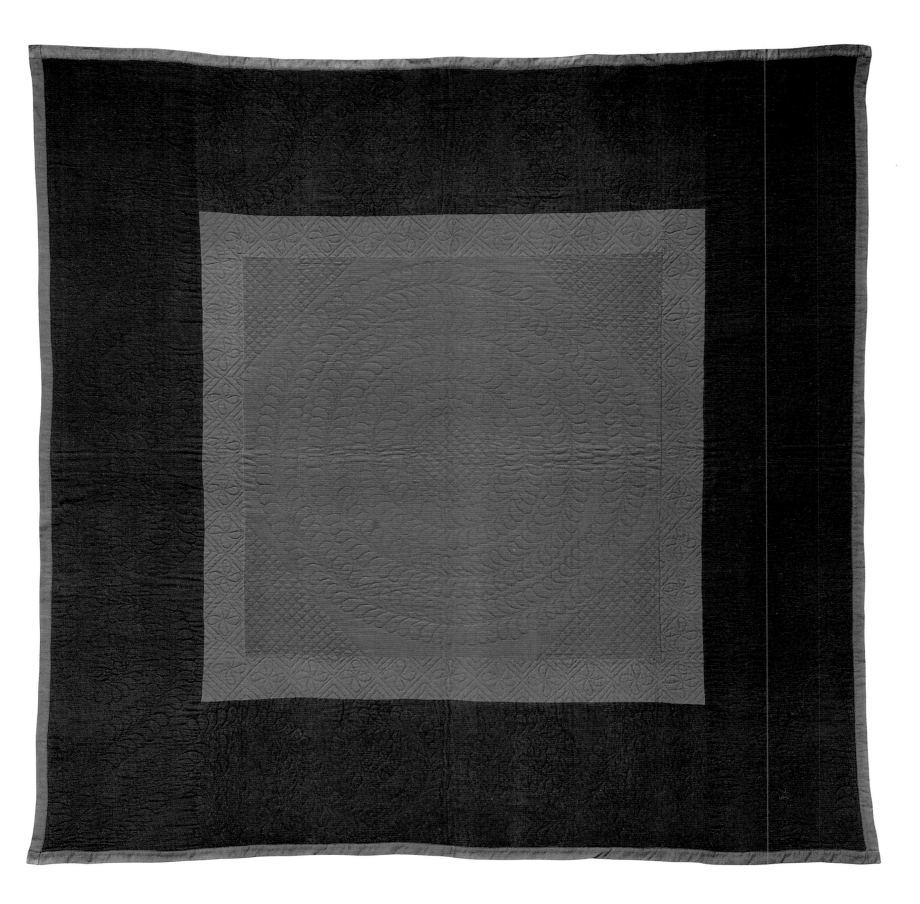

3

Center Square

*Unknown Amish quiltmaker, American, Lancaster County, Pennsylvania, Circa 1890, Pieced wools, 77 x 77 inches, 585.187*

A central concept in Amish life is to be *in* but not *of* the world. The Amish are enjoined to be different from the "English" (their term for people outside the Amish faith) culture surrounding them. Dress and appearance are two of the most important ways they distinguish themselves; their quilts, too, cannot be confused with others. Many American quilts of this period are much more decorative, intricately pieced of pastel-colored, floral-printed fabrics.

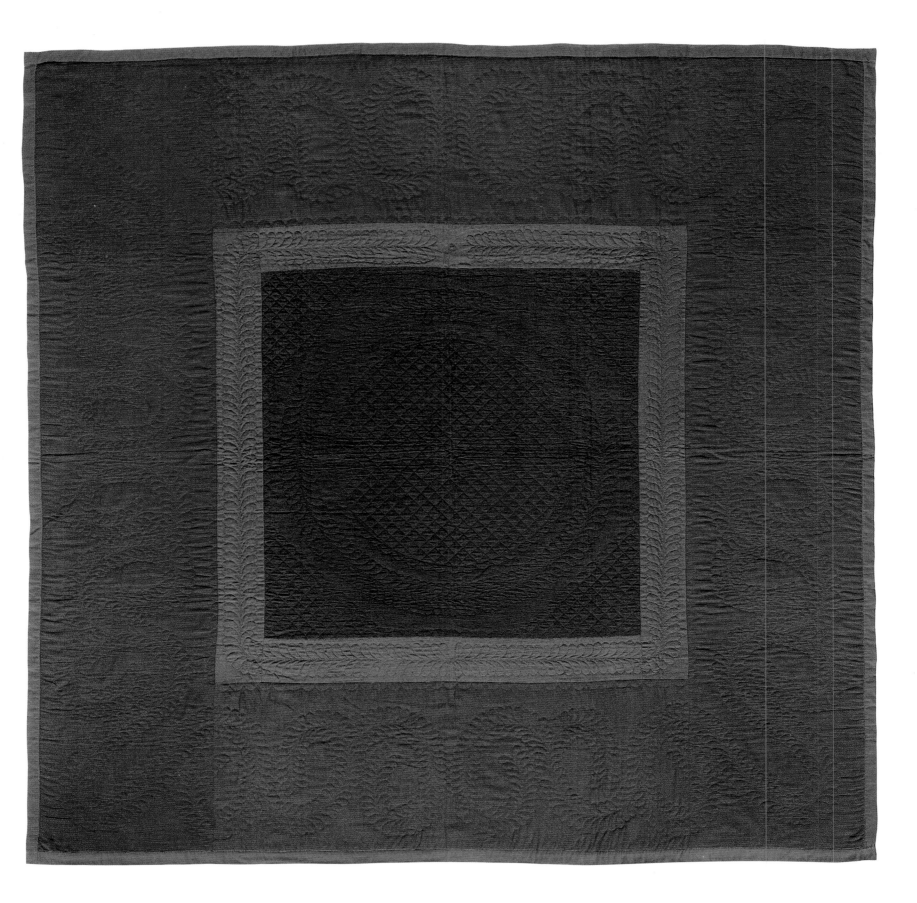

4

## Center Square

*Unknown Amish quiltmaker, American, Lancaster County, Pennsylvania, Circa 1920, Pieced wools, 74 x 74 inches, 585.271*

It is unusual to find this design made so late. By the 1920s, most Lancaster women were adding a square on point to the center to create the extremely popular Diamond in the Square. The interior quilting in this Center Square, purchased from an Amish farm near Peach Bottom in the southern part of Lancaster County, is far plainer than in the earlier examples illustrated in the preceding plates (Plates 1–3).

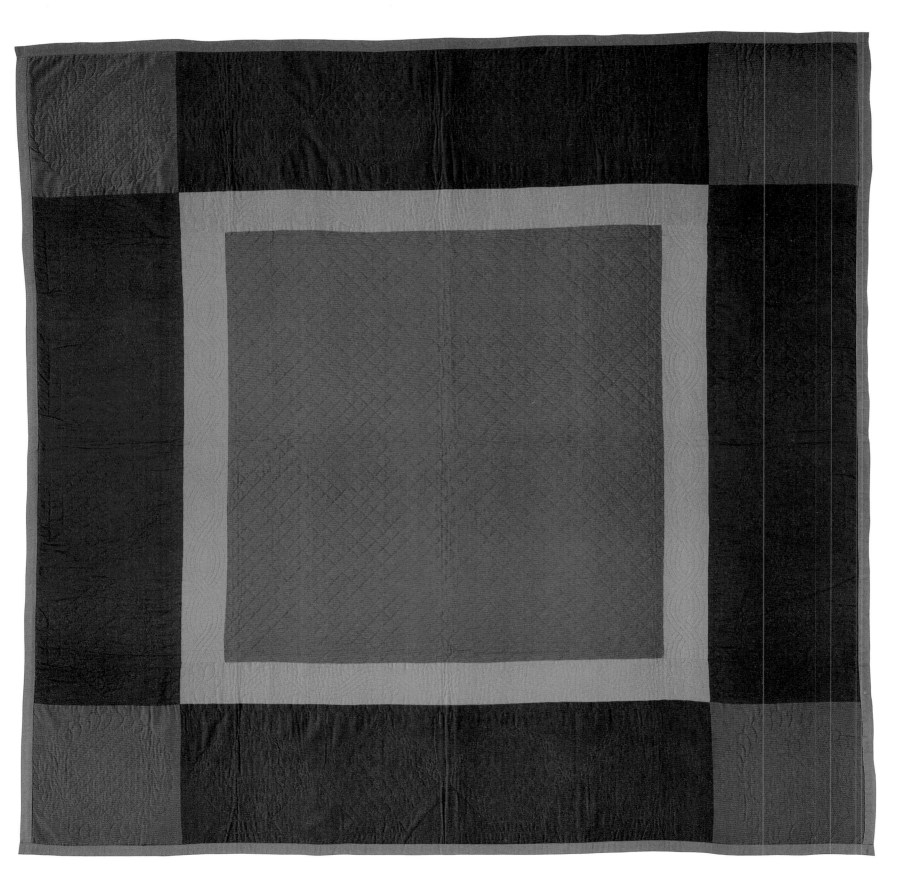

5

### D i a m o n d   i n   t h e   S q u a r e

*Unknown Amish quiltmaker, American, Lancaster County, Pennsylvania, Circa 1910–20, Pieced wools, 81 x 81 inches, 585.275*

Lancaster County Amish women loved the elegantly simple Diamond in the Square pattern and made it
again and again from the late nineteenth century through the 1960s. Because it was so popular with them and only they made it,
Diamond is the pattern most closely associated with the Amish in Lancaster County.
This piece was purchased in Intercourse, Pennsylvania, from an Amish woman who observed that the quilting in it is
"exceptional, even for an Amish quilt."

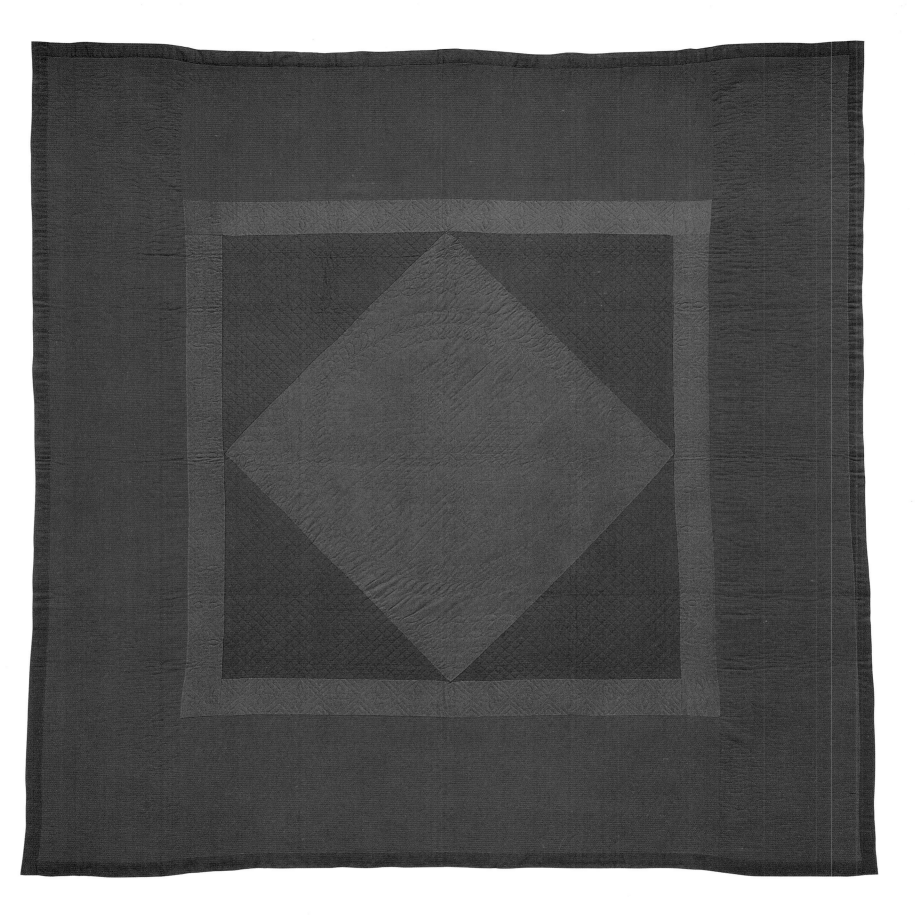

Diamond in the Square

*Unknown Amish quiltmaker, American, Lancaster County, Pennsylvania, Circa 1900, Pieced wools, 78 x 78 inches, 585.270*

The Amish are conservative in a cultural sense: they are uncomfortable with change. A traditional culture, they prefer the old to the new in both their religious and their social lives, so the Lancaster County Amish made only a few quilt patterns and variations on those patterns. Within very strict limitations of form, however, Amish quiltmakers made personal aesthetic decisions regarding colors, color placement, quilting and format.

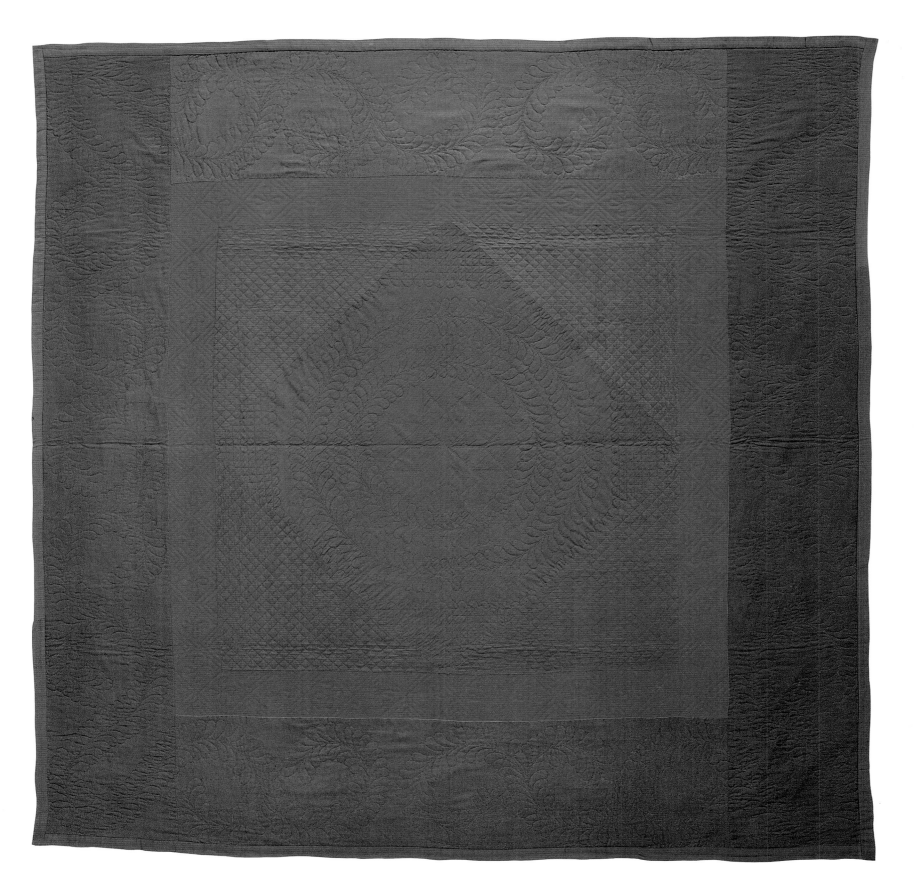

Diamond in the Square

*Unknown Amish quiltmaker, American, Lancaster County, Pennsylvania, Circa 1920–30, Pieced wools, 76 x 76 inches, 585.196*

The Amish were discouraged from using printed fabrics and from engaging in the "worldly" practice of using many small pieces in their quilts.
Among quilts of all the many Amish groups, Lancaster County's are especially spare.
In this Diamond, there is a slight change in hue in the vertical and horizontal wide borders, probably related to the nap of the wool.
When the fabric is turned, it catches the light differently, appearing a slightly different shade.

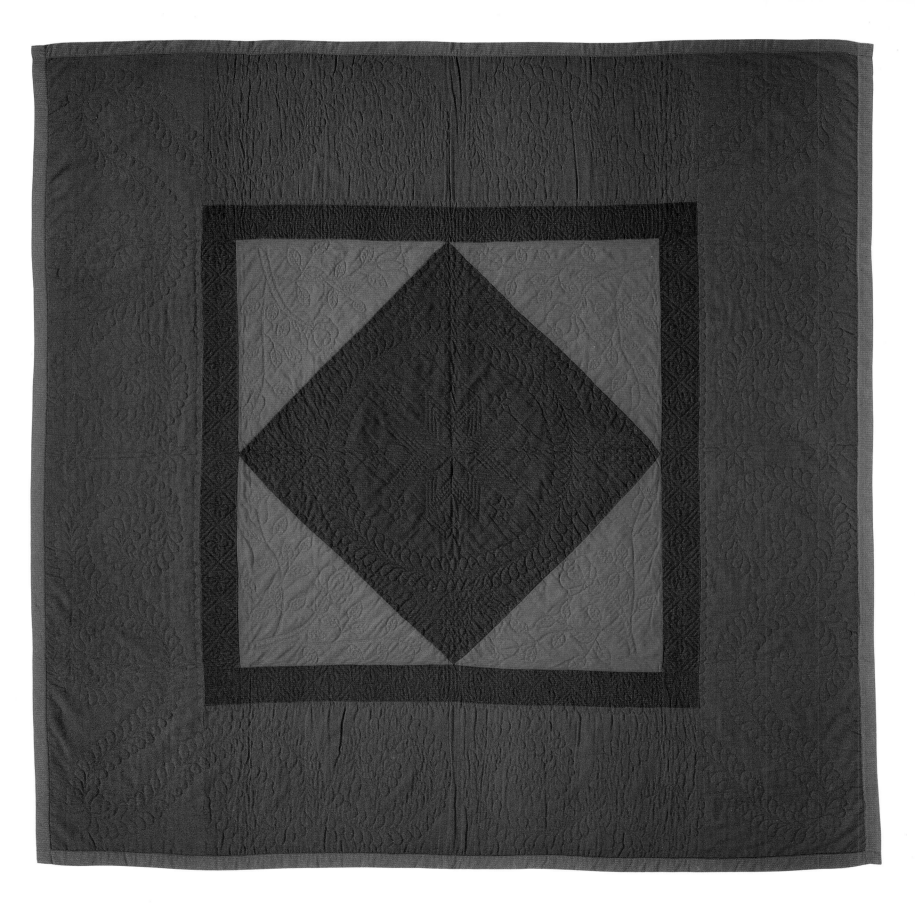

8

Diamond in the Square

*Unknown Amish quiltmaker, American, Lancaster County, Pennsylvania, Circa 1920, Pieced wools, 78 x 78 inches, 585.103*

This is a very pure example of the simple Diamond, the essence perhaps. Here we see the intense,
glowing colors for which twentieth-century Lancaster quilts are known.
Some students of Lancaster society report that the Amish sometimes call the Diamond design "Cape," or in their dialect "Halstuch," a reference
to the shape of the traditional shawl the women wear over their shoulders. (McCauley, *Decorative Arts of the Amish of Lancaster County*,
caption p. 12; Granick, *The Amish Quilt*, 76.)

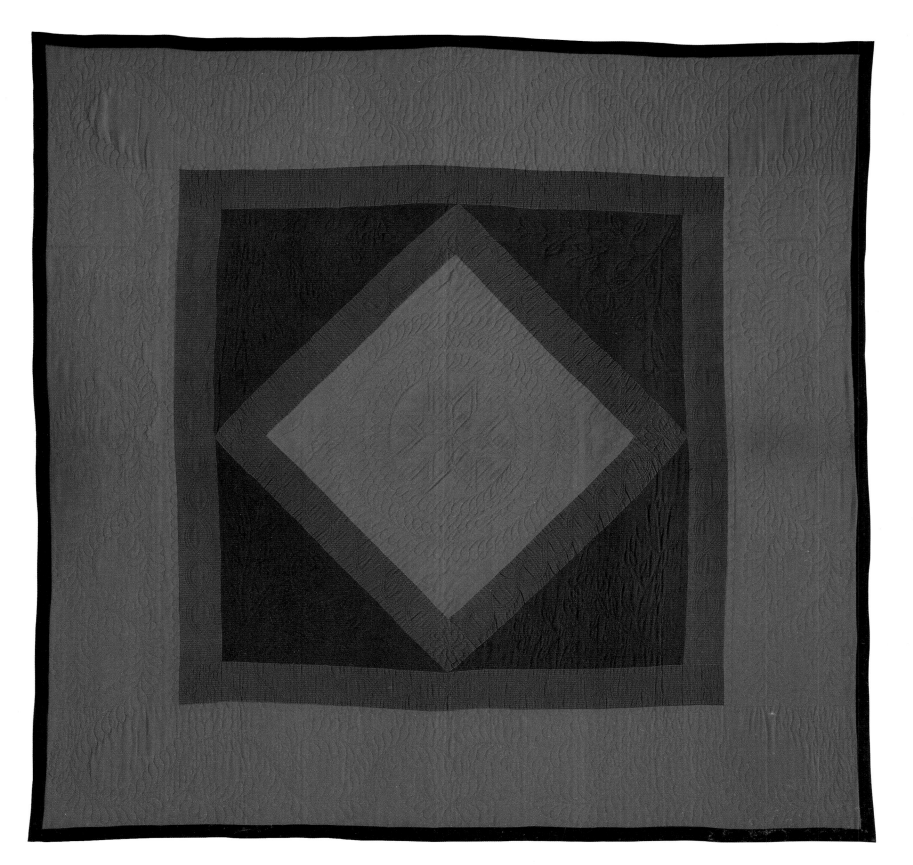

Diamond in the Square

*Unknown Amish quiltmaker, American, Lancaster County, Pennsylvania, Circa 1920–30, Pieced wools, 76 x 76 inches, 585.168*

Obedience is a fundamental principle guiding Amish life. Individuals submit to the authority of the group and willingly accept community-determined standards. In their quilts, almost all Lancaster County Amish women conform to a conventional format: a central design sits within a narrow inner border and a wider outer border finished with an added binding, usually of a contrasting color.

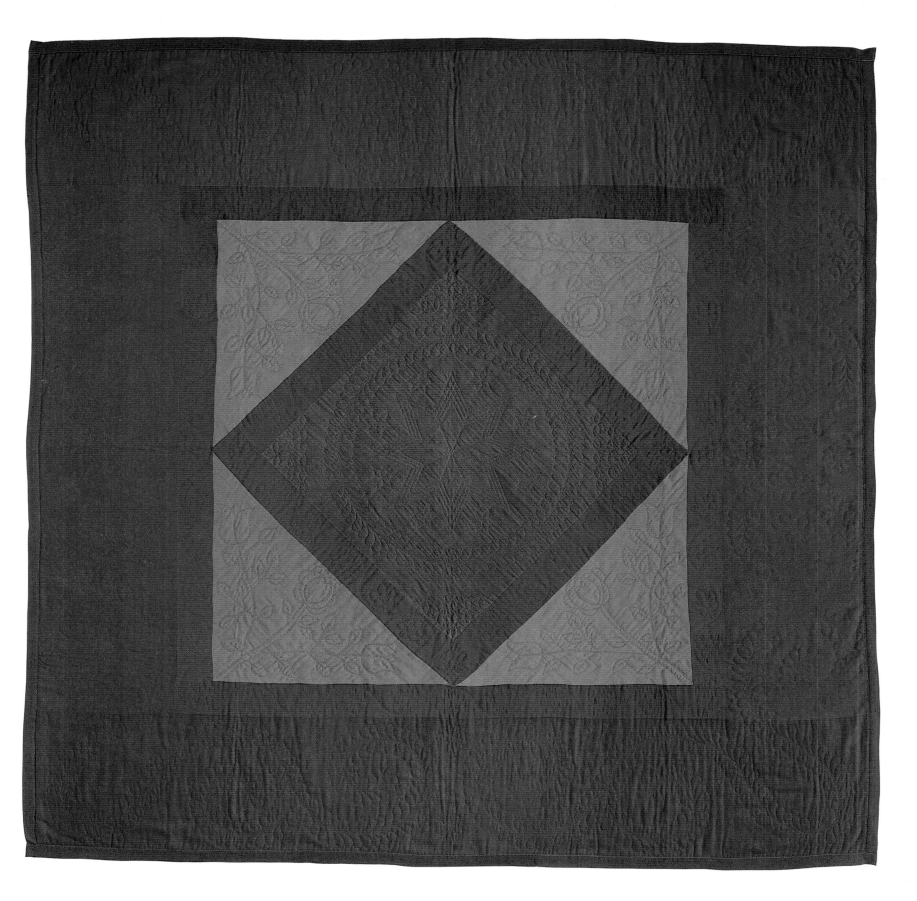

## Sawtooth Diamond

*Made by Sarah Zook, Amish quiltmaker, American, Lancaster County, Pennsylvania, Dated in quilting: "1925," Pieced wools, 82 x 82 inches, 585.214*

Sawtooth was one of the variations on the basic Diamond, though it is seen rather infrequently. This marvelously crafted example was very carefully planned to perfectly balance the Sawtooth edgings. The quilted "feathers" in the blue diamond also come to an elegant resolution.
While it is customary for some Amish women in the Midwest to sign their quilts with initials, the "SZ" quilted into this Lancaster piece is an exception.

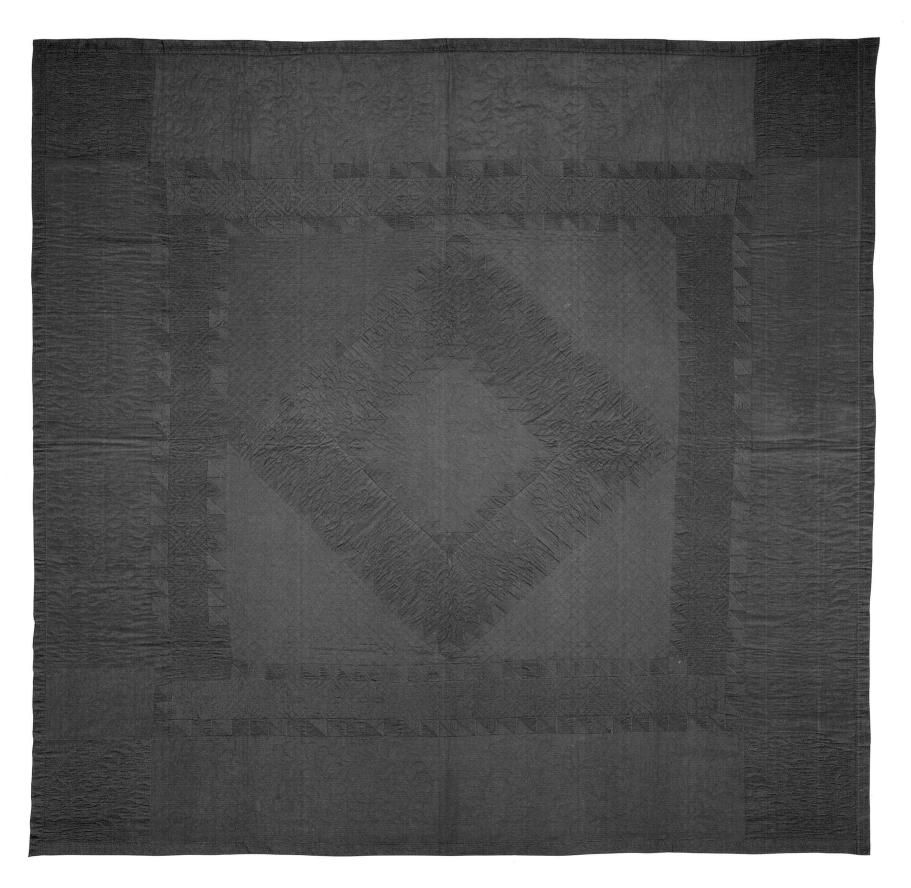

11

Diamond in the Square

*Unknown Amish quiltmaker, American, Lancaster County, Pennsylvania, Circa 1920, Pieced wools, 77 x 77 inches, 585.126*

Wool absorbs dyes in an especially concentrated way and provided Lancaster women with their particular, lush palette. Here is a
superb example of the essential Diamond in the rich jewel tones Lancaster women of this period loved. Elaborate, sweeping quilting designs balance
the stark geometry of the piecing in Lancaster quilts.

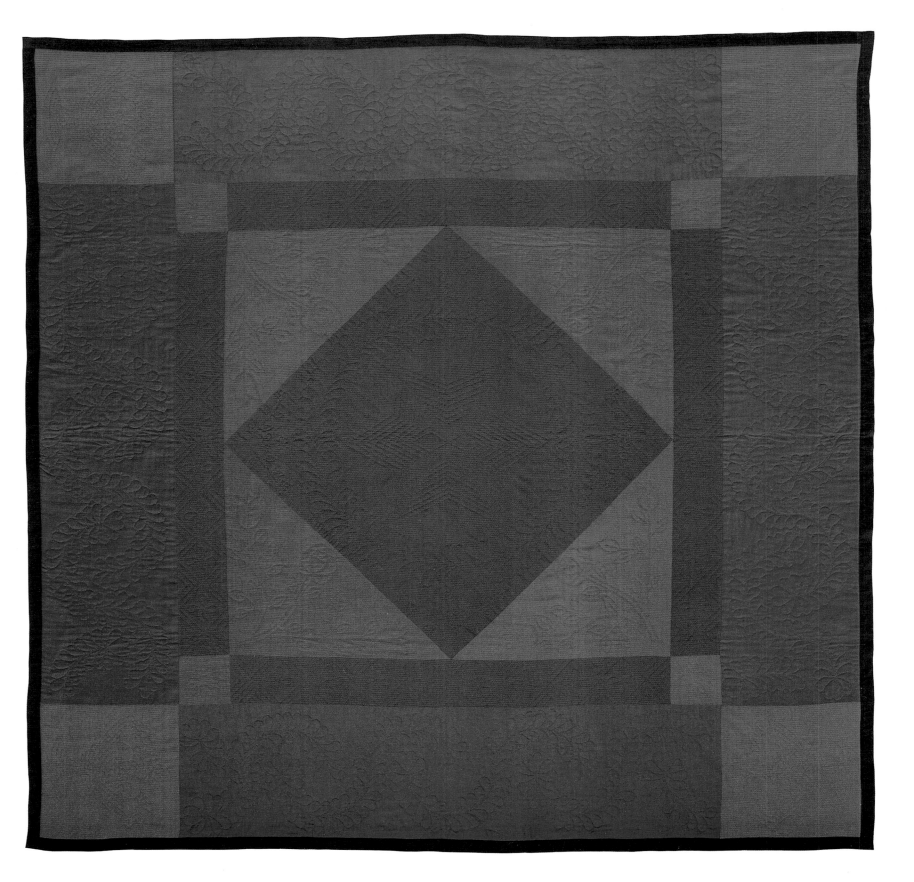

12

# Diamond in the Square

*Unknown Amish quiltmaker, American, Lancaster County, Pennsylvania, Circa 1920–30, Pieced wools, 74 x 74 inches, 585.280*

The daughter of the woman who made this quilt said that "the dark blue henrietta was from my mother's dress."
The Lancaster Amish use the term "henrietta" to describe a variety of fabrics, but it usually refers to the fine wools they favor for their quilts.
Lancaster quilts are most often square and symmetrically arranged, almost always ranging from 72 to 88 inches square.

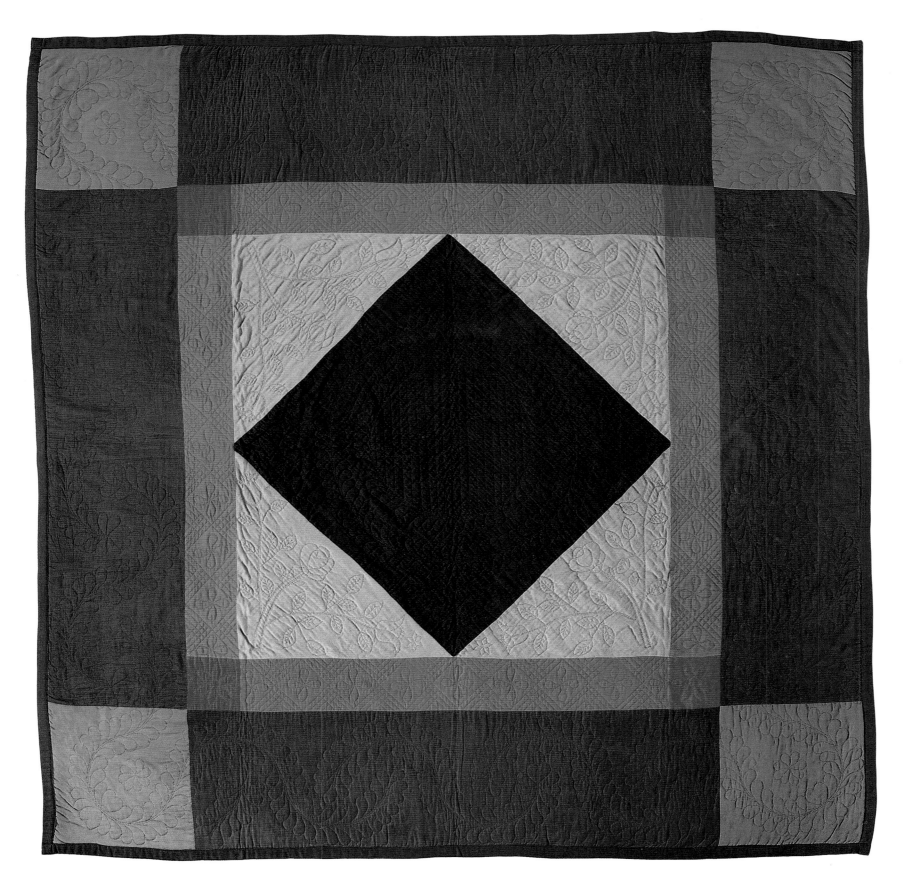

# Diamond in the Square

*Unknown Amish quiltmaker, American, Lancaster County, Pennsylvania, Circa 1920, Pieced wools and rayons, 80 x 80 inches, 585.282*

Within a prescribed format, one option Lancaster women had was to make their quilts more or less complex by adding various combinations of "frames" and corner blocks. In this book, we have arranged the Diamonds in order of increasing complexity. Compare this "fully developed" example first with the Center Square quilts (Plates 1–4) and with the preceding Diamonds, starting with Plate 5.

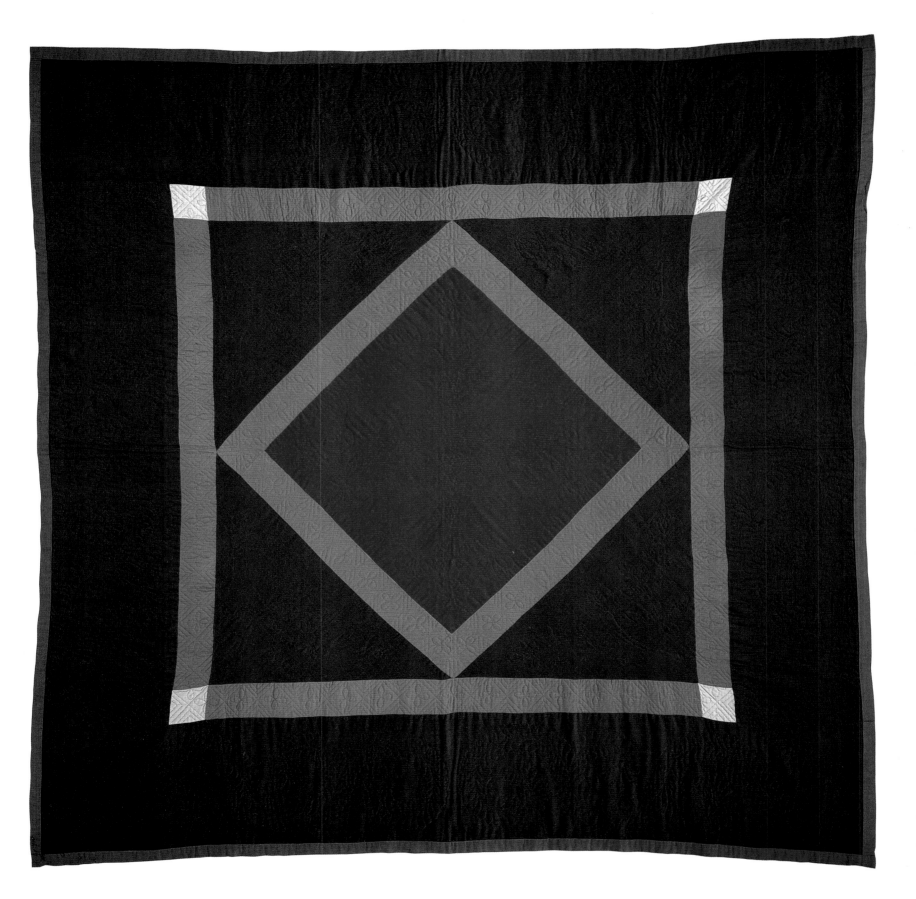

Diamond in the Square

*Unknown Amish quiltmaker, American, Lancaster County, Pennsylvania, Circa 1940, Pieced wools and rayons, 80 x 80 inches, 585.227*

Later Lancaster quilts are often quilted in floral rather than geometric or abstract designs. They are also typically less densely quilted than their predecessors. One contributing factor may be that it is more difficult to make tiny, fine quilting stitches in the synthetic fabrics Amish women were using in the later period. Much of the entire Lancaster County Amish quilting vocabulary can be seen in this plate and the three following.

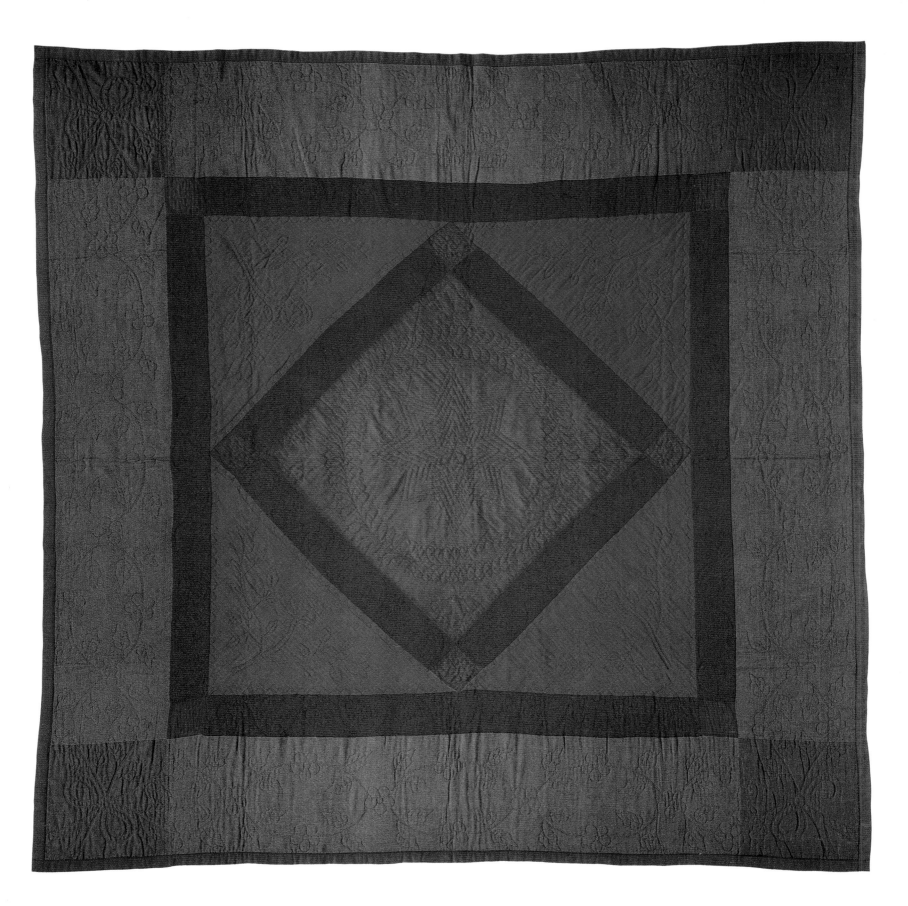

Diamond in the Square

*Unknown Amish quiltmaker, American, Lancaster County, Pennsylvania, Circa 1910, Pieced wools, 78 x 78 inches, 585.212*

This splendid quilt can be seen as transitional in its use of color. The brown belongs to an early period before the turn of the century;
the other colors are drawn from the sumptuous palette used a bit later. An expanded range of colors became available to Amish women after 1900;
by the 1920s Lancaster quilts were filled with intense, relatively bright hues.

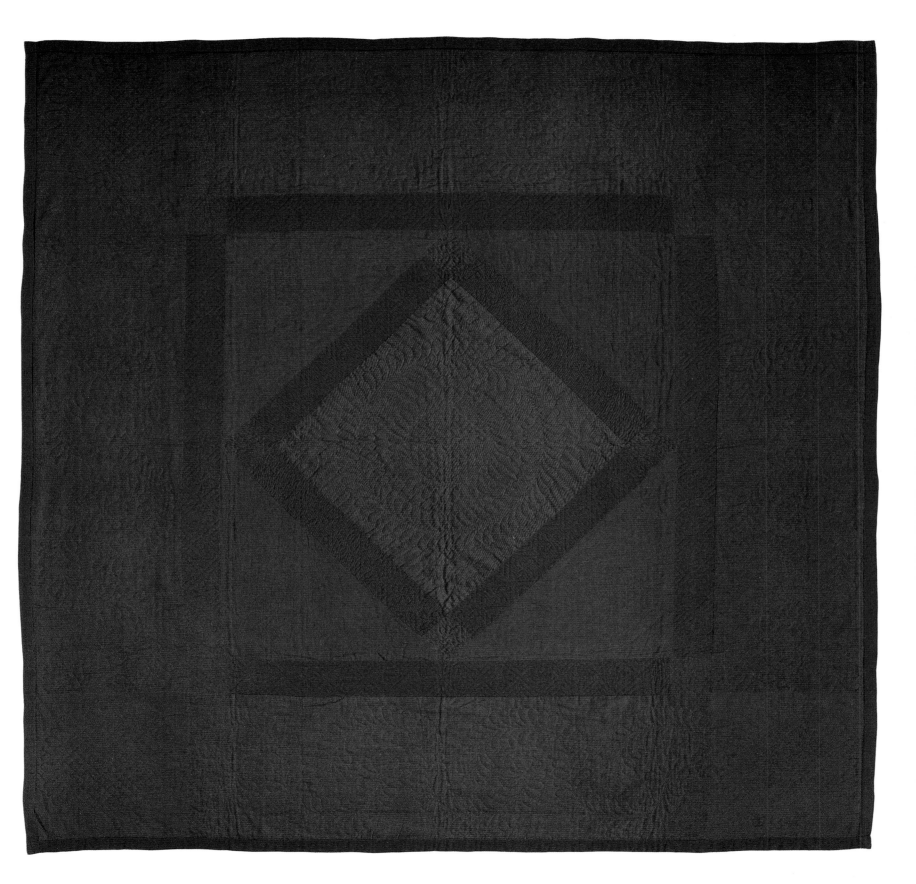

## D i a m o n d   i n   t h e   S q u a r e

*Unknown Amish quiltmaker, American, Lancaster County, Pennsylvania, Circa 1920–30, Pieced wools, 77 x 77 inches, 585.167*

The popularity of the simple Diamond among Lancaster quiltmakers is reflected in the Esprit collection.
This is one of our more than thirty examples, fourteen of which are illustrated here.
This Diamond has a clear, almost sparkling feeling, which the quiltmaker achieved by her particular arrangement of color.
Compare the use of red by this quiltmaker with that in the next plate.

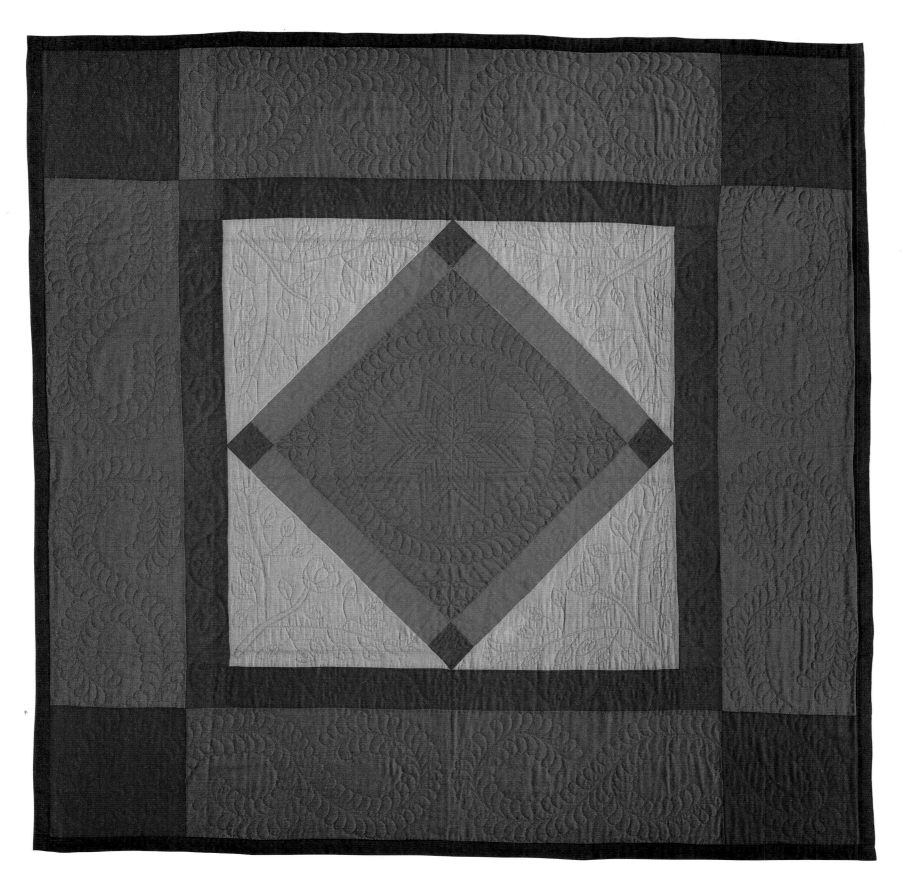

Diamond in the Square

*Unknown Amish quiltmaker, American, Lancaster County, Pennsylvania, Circa 1930–40, Pieced wools, 79 x 81 inches, 585.002*

The colors and bordering elements are two of the few areas where the Amish quiltmaker could express her own personality.
Within the context of a highly codified framework, these choices take on a great deal of importance. In this Diamond, the quiltmaker pretty much
"went to the limit" by combining seven colors and adding frames, borders and corners at her every opportunity.

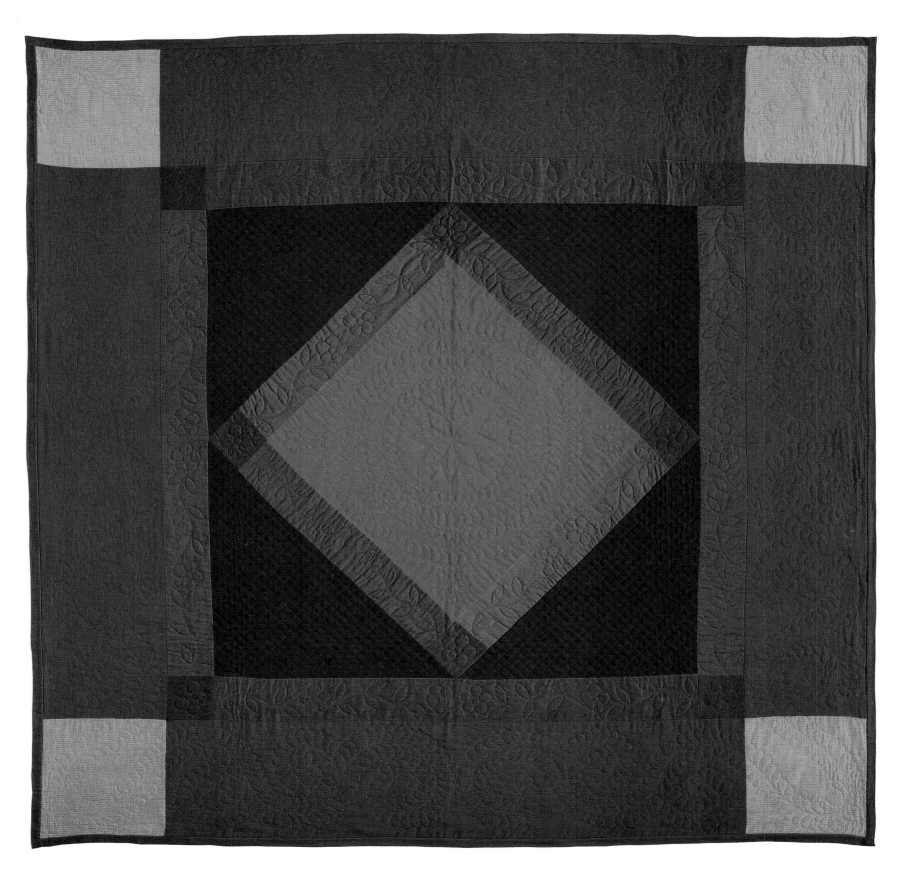

## D i a m o n d   i n   t h e   S q u a r e

*Unknown Amish quiltmaker, American, Lancaster County, Pennsylvania, Circa 1930–40, Pieced wools, 79 x 79 inches, 585.105*

The colors we outsiders tend to associate with the Amish are the dark tones of their overclothing—
the black, navy or charcoal of their coats and capes. In fact, the Amish were permitted quite a range of color, as long as the cloth was unprinted.
Women's and children's clothing was particularly colorful. Quilts were made from the same fabrics used in their apparel.
In this quilt, the usually strongly defined points of the inner Diamond recede because the quiltmaker used a light green in the corner blocks.

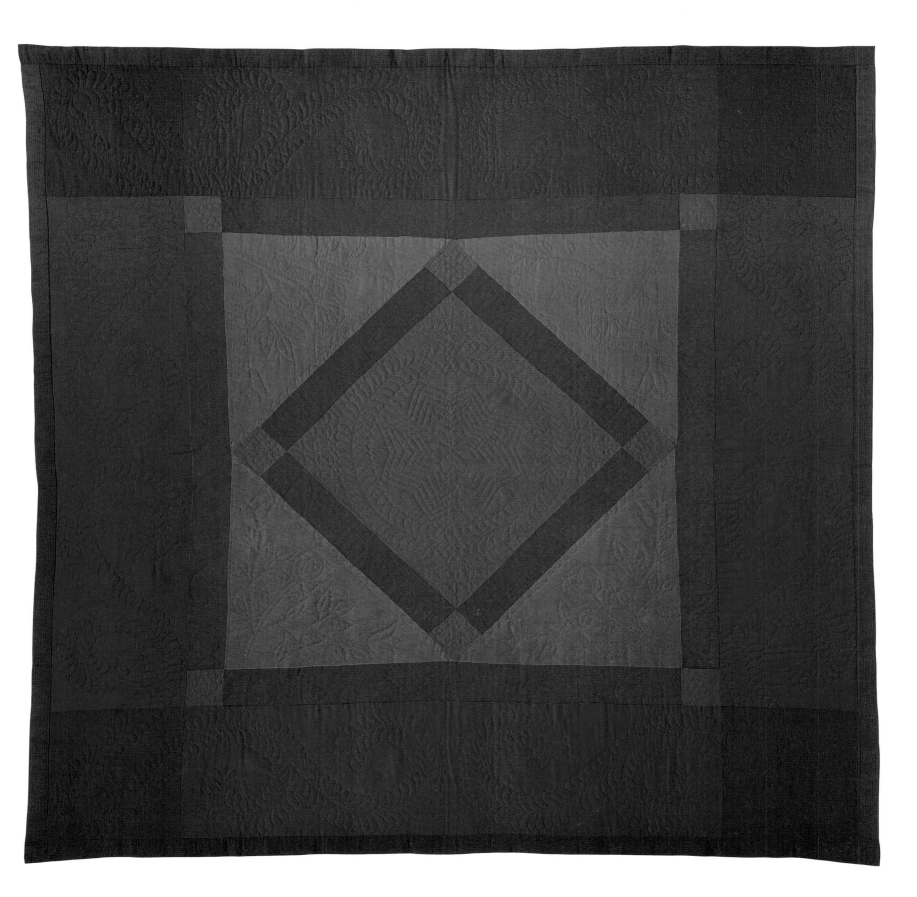

Diamond in the Square

*Unknown Amish quiltmaker, American, Lancaster County, Pennsylvania, Dated in quilting: "1921," Pieced wools, 76 x 76 inches, 585.250*

This is the only example we've seen of a Diamond with a second inner border.
The maker also distinguished herself by rounding the outer corners and by modifying traditional quilting designs.
The basic principles by which the Amish live have remained basically unchanged since the sixteenth century, and are contained in a book called the
*Ordnung.* Contemporary rules within each district are primarily unwritten and apply to the customs of daily life. There are few specific references
to quiltmaking; the understanding of what is acceptable in quiltmaking comes down to "commonly held perceptions."
(Granick, *The Amish Quilt,* 81.)

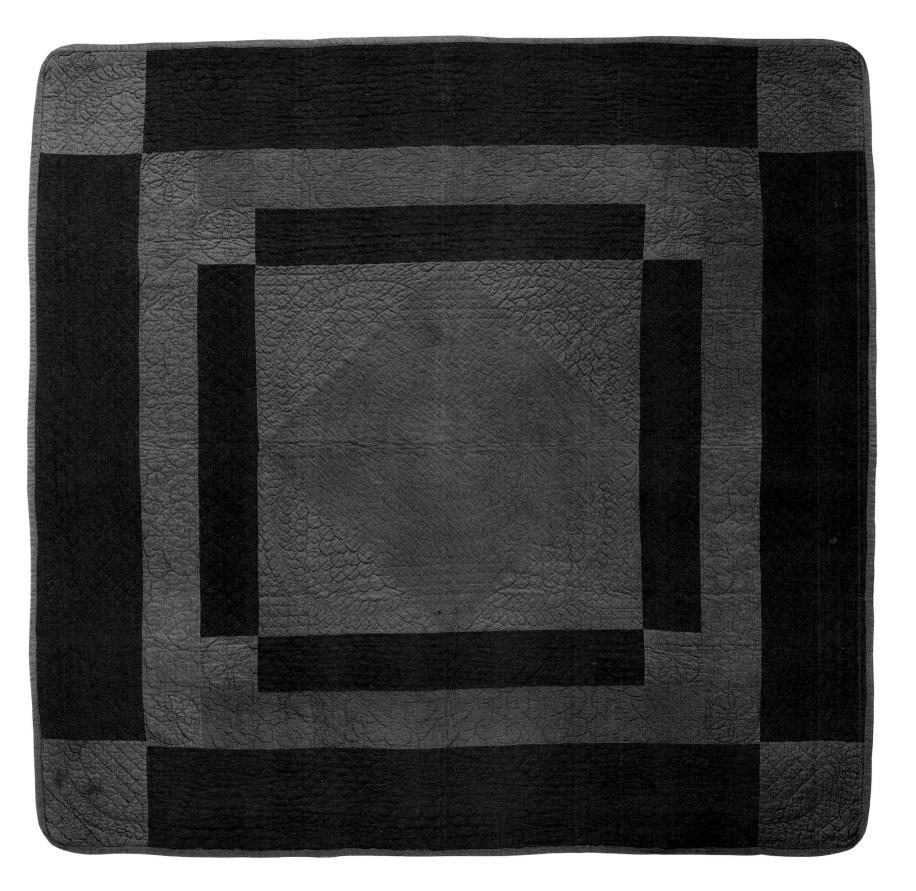

## Diamond in the Square

*Variation*

*Unknown Amish quiltmaker, American, Lancaster County, Pennsylvania, Circa 1910, Pieced wools, 72 x 72 inches, 585.190*

We find adaptations and combinations of traditional patterns, rather than wholly new designs, in Amish quilts. In quiltmaking, as in all of Amish life, behavior that reinforces a sense of unity and fellowship is more highly valued than an individual's innovation or achievement. Although each of the two patterns combined here was exceedingly popular in Lancaster Amish quilts, we have seen only one other example of Diamond filled with Ninepatch.

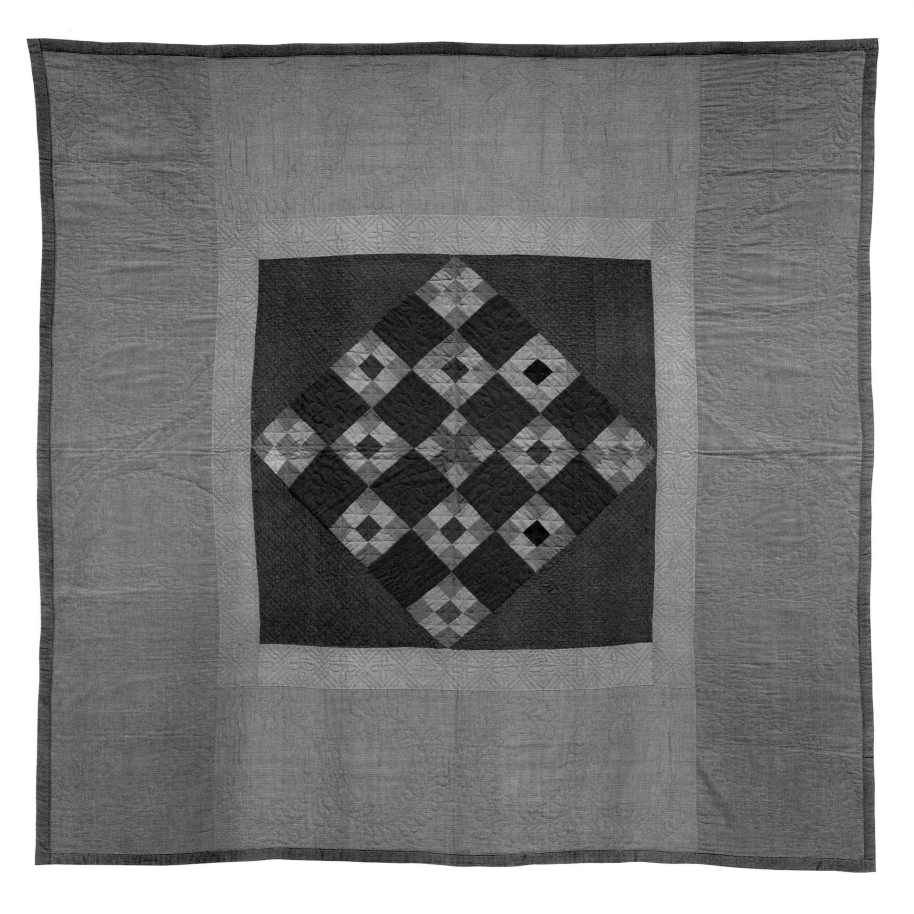

## Diamond in the Square
*Variation*

*Unknown Amish quiltmaker, American, Lancaster County, Pennsylvania, Circa 1930, Pieced wools and rayons, 76 x 76 inches, 585.016*

At Esprit, we are always on the lookout for successful examples of quilts with uncommon treatments. Here, a design known as Trip Around the World
sits within a simple, traditional Diamond. A subtle variant of the familiar Sunshine and Shadow design,
Trip Around the World is made up of squares set on point, rather than on square. For comparison, see Plate 33.

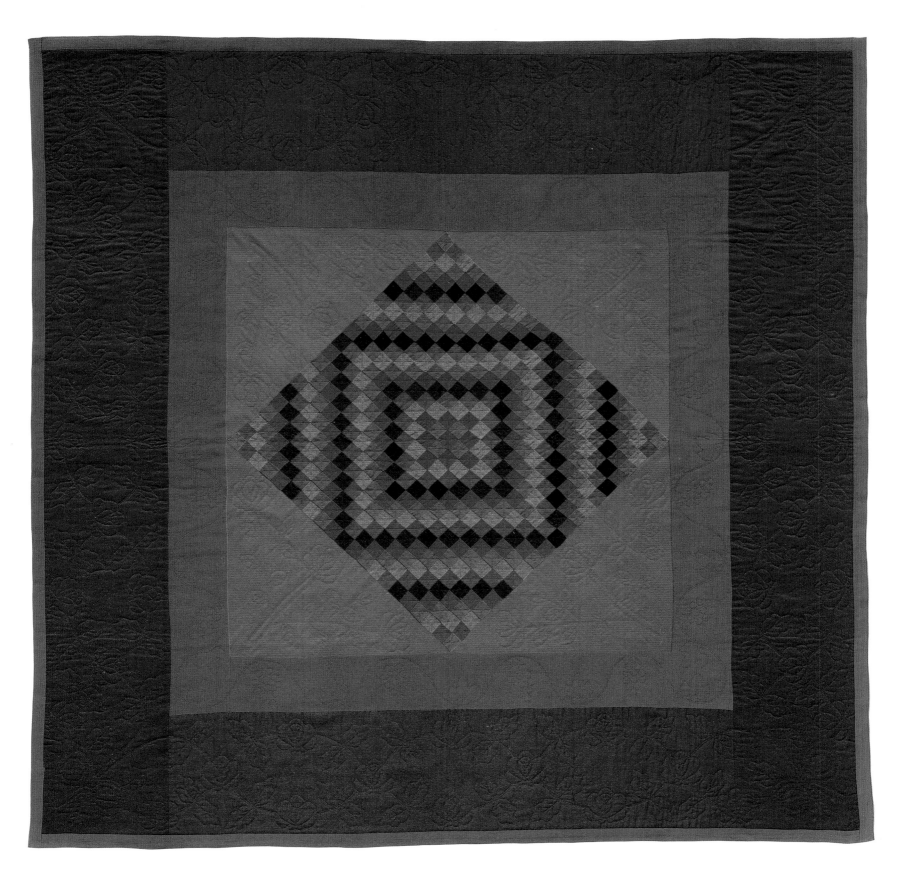

D i a m o n d   i n   t h e   S q u a r e
*Variation*
*Unknown Amish quiltmaker, American, Lancaster County, Pennsylvania, Circa 1930–40, Pieced wools and rayons, 78 x 79 inches, 585.068*

As in the larger American culture, quiltmaking for the Amish is inextricably bound to apparel. Clothing scraps were sometimes used, but in Lancaster, fabric was often purchased specifically for quilts. By the time the Amish came to quiltmaking in the middle of the nineteenth century, it was generally not necessary to weave or dye cloth at home; commercially manufactured fabrics were readily available.

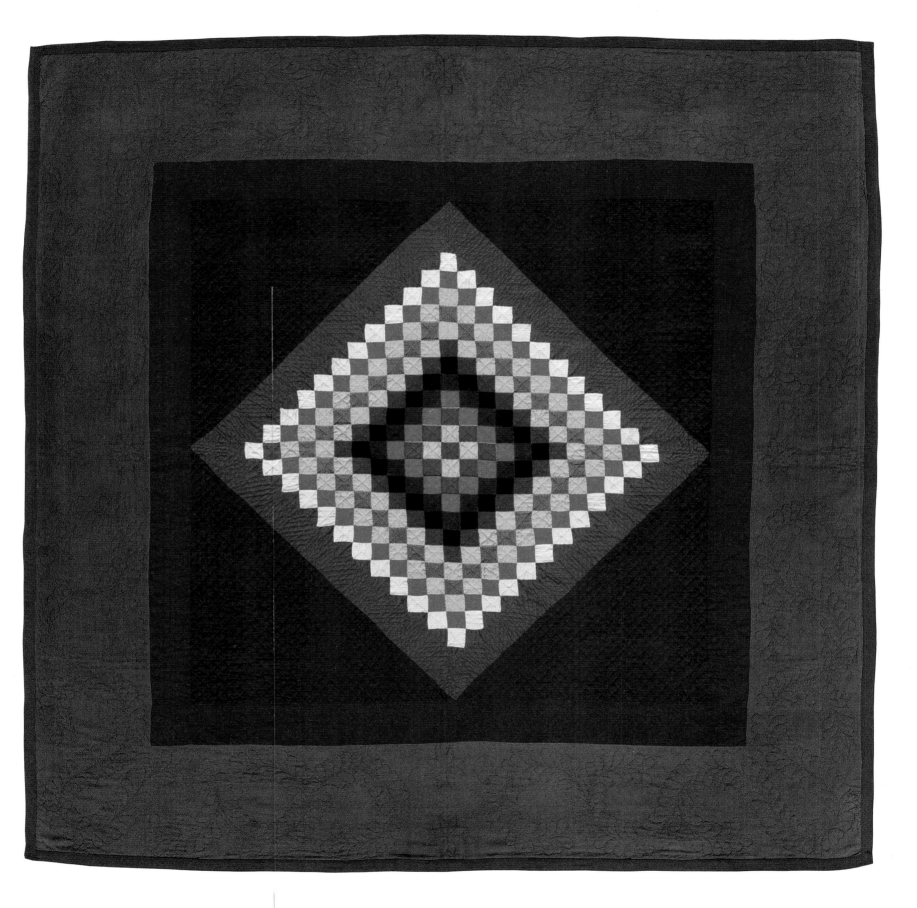

## D i a m o n d   i n   t h e   S q u a r e
*Variation*
*Unknown Amish quiltmaker, American, Lancaster County, Pennsylvania, Circa 1940, Pieced wools, 74 x 74 inches, 585.267*

Amish women had access to an abundance of marvelous new colors as dyeing and setting techniques improved in the twentieth century.
Later Lancaster quilts can have astonishing associations of colors.
Synthetic fabrics became available soon after the turn of the century; rayon was domestically produced as early as 1910. (Granick, *The Amish Quilt*, 47.)
Throughout the thirties and forties, man-made fibers were commonly included in Lancaster quilts.

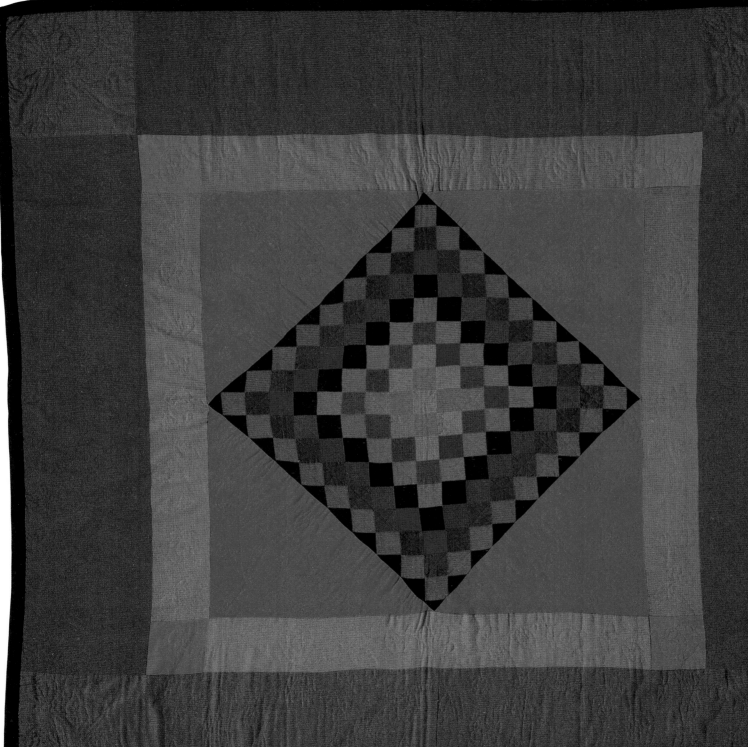

## D i a m o n d   i n   t h e   S q u a r e
### *Variation*

*Unknown Amish quiltmaker, American, Lancaster County, Pennsylvania, Circa 1930, Pieced wools and cottons, 79 x 79 inches, 585.072*

Although there are several quilts in the Esprit collection that combine Sunshine and Shadow and Diamond in the Square, this treatment
is actually quite uncommon in Lancaster quilts.
Here, in addition to the multicolored center, the quiltmaker used seven colors and added every possible border and corner.
Compare this with a similar quilt in Plate 22, which has no corners.

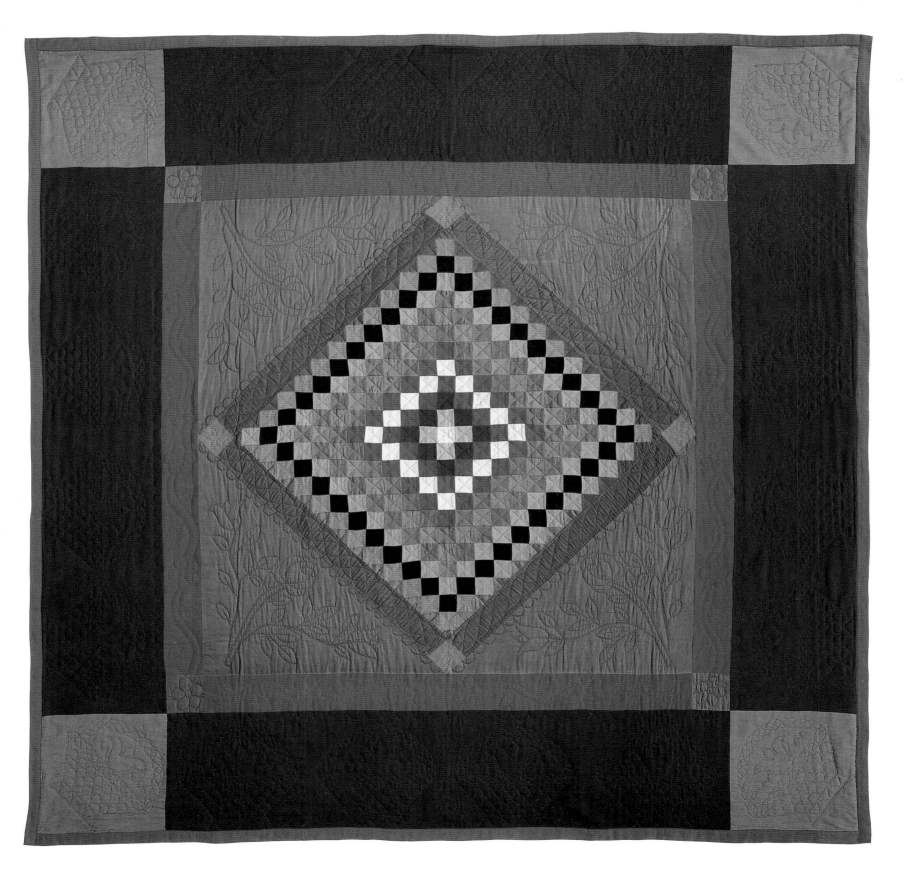

## Diamond in the Square
### *Variation*
*Unknown Amish quiltmaker, American, Lancaster County, Pennsylvania, Circa 1940, Pieced wools, 79 x 81 inches, 585.272*

Intrinsically conservative, the Lancaster Amish are slow to change old ways. We can see this in their quilts:
they maintained into the 1960s a style of construction (the so-called central-medallion format) generally abandoned by mainstream American quiltmakers
by 1850. The Lancaster Amish favor quilts based on a single central design element, such as the Diamond, surrounded by multiple borders.
This quilt was found in northern Lancaster County, near Lebanon.

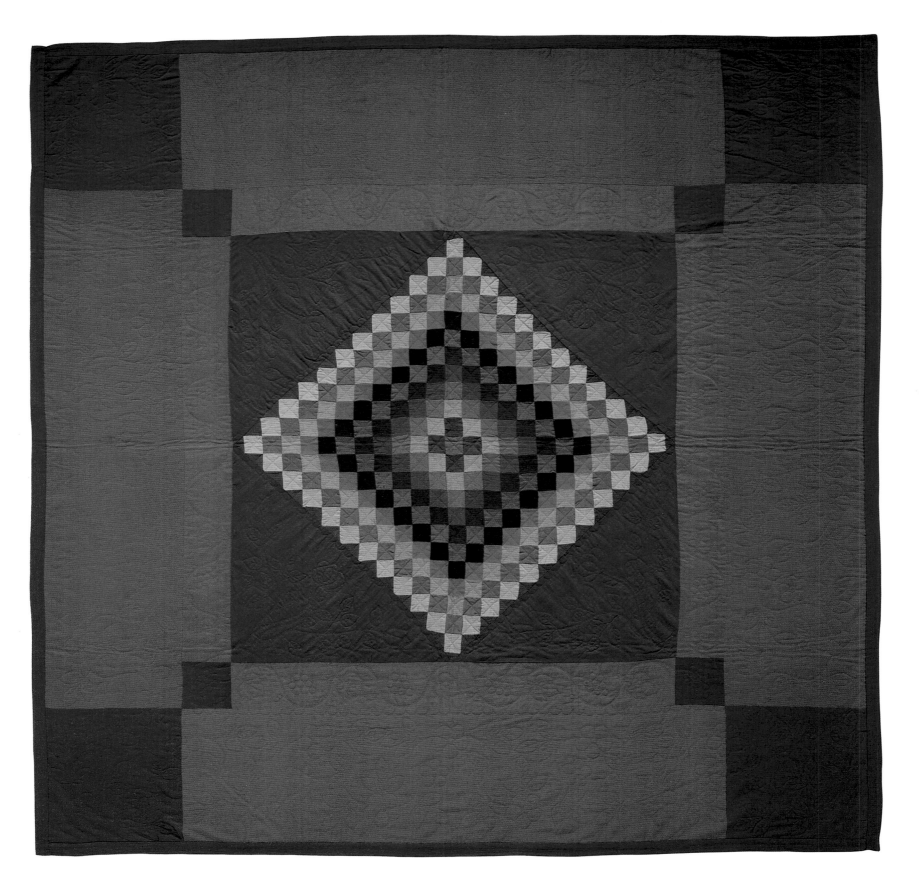

D i a m o n d   i n   t h e   S q u a r e
*Variation*
*Made by Fanny Petersheim, Amish quiltmaker, American, Lancaster County, Pennsylvania, Circa 1920, Pieced wools and rayons,*
*90 x 90 inches, 585.110*

Fanny Petersheim (1879–1941) left us a most unusual quilt—a Diamond filled with a design called Philadelphia Pavement,
a series of little Sunshine and Shadows. The central design becomes a bit more orderly when looked at from an angle, but it is still far more "askew"
than most Lancaster quilts, known for their symmetry and precision.

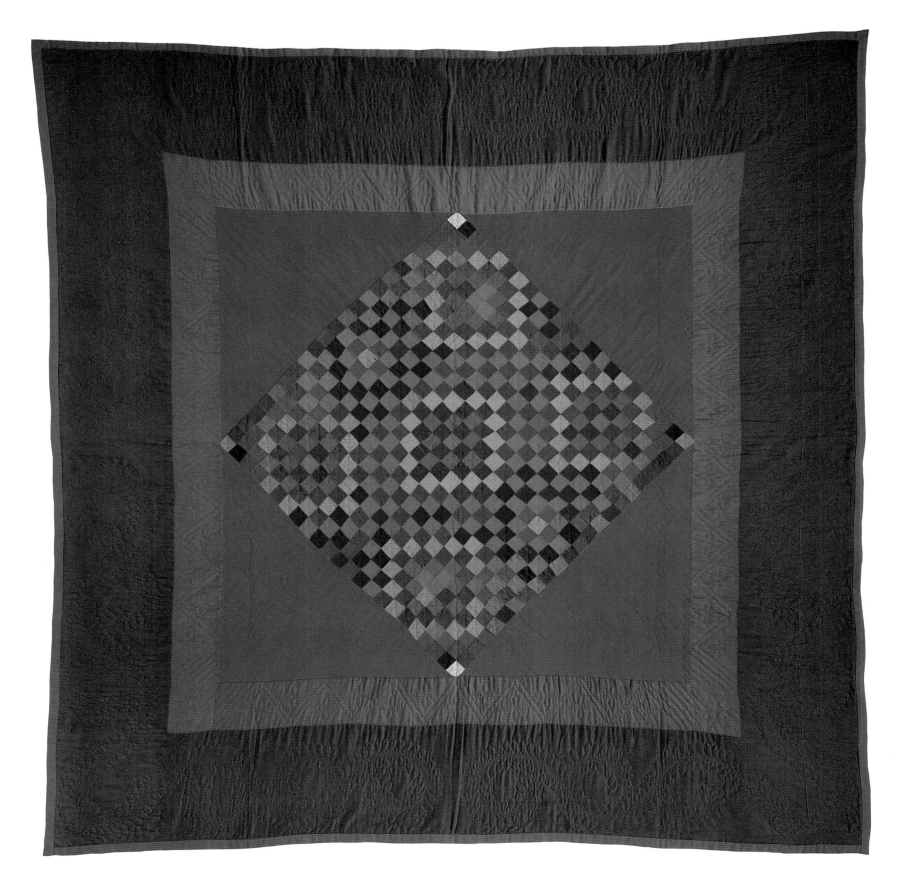

D i a m o n d   i n   t h e   S q u a r e
*Variation*
*Made by Katie Stoltzfus, Amish quiltmaker, American, Lancaster County, Pennsylvania, Circa 1927, Pieced wools, 72 x 72 inches, 585.288*

At Esprit, we almost never purchase quilts directly from the Amish and only rarely are given histories on acquisitions.
This time, we learned just a little bit more than usual. Katie Stoltzfus made this rather eccentric piece around 1927, combining four common
Lancaster County elements—Diamond, Ninepatch, Bars and Sawtooth—into a unique interpretation of the Diamond.

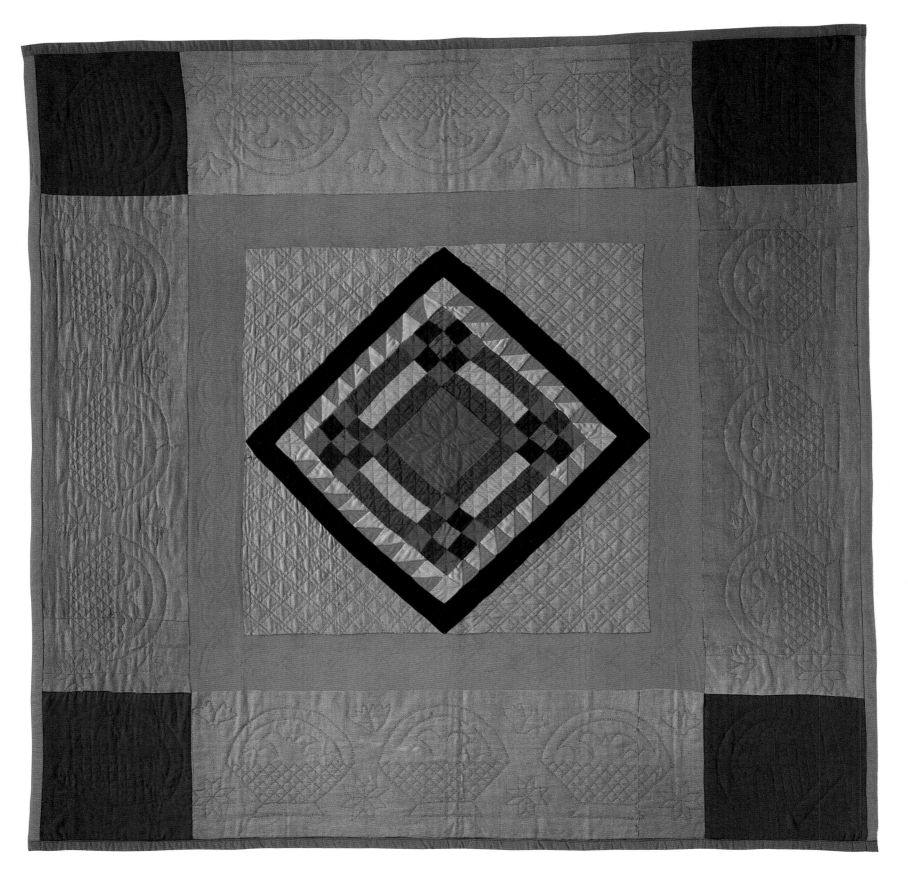

S u n s h i n e   a n d   S h a d o w
*Variation*
*Unknown Amish quiltmaker, American, Lancaster County, Pennsylvania, Circa 1900–20, Pieced wools and cottons, 74 x 80 inches, 585.009*

This is the only time we have seen the reverse of the configuration illustrated in Plates 19–22.
Here the Diamond is set *inside* the Sunshine and Shadow. Other subtle touches of the quiltmaker's personal mark appear in her choice of quilting designs:
the tiny baskets quilted into the pink center and the lyres stitched into the corners are unusual.

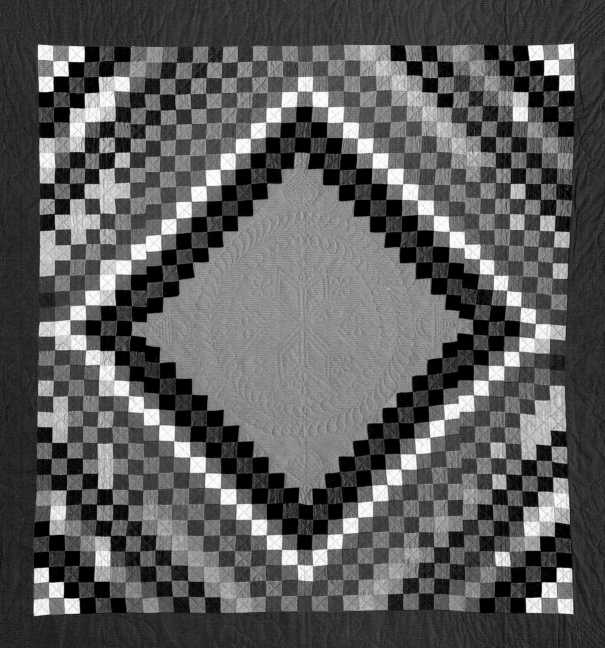

29

D i a m o n d   i n   t h e   S q u a r e
*Variation*
*Unknown Amish quiltmaker, American, Lancaster County, Pennsylvania, Circa 1930, Pieced wools and rayons, 76 x 76 inches, 585.216*

We have seen only one other quilt in which the quiltmaker integrated these three designs—
Diamond, Sunshine and Shadow and Grandmother's Dream (also called Trip Around the World; see Plate 21).
The joining of two or more traditional designs (as seen in Plates 20–29) is about as far as Lancaster Amish quiltmakers went in terms of innovation.
Committed to their traditional ways, they are among the least experimental of all the Amish groups.

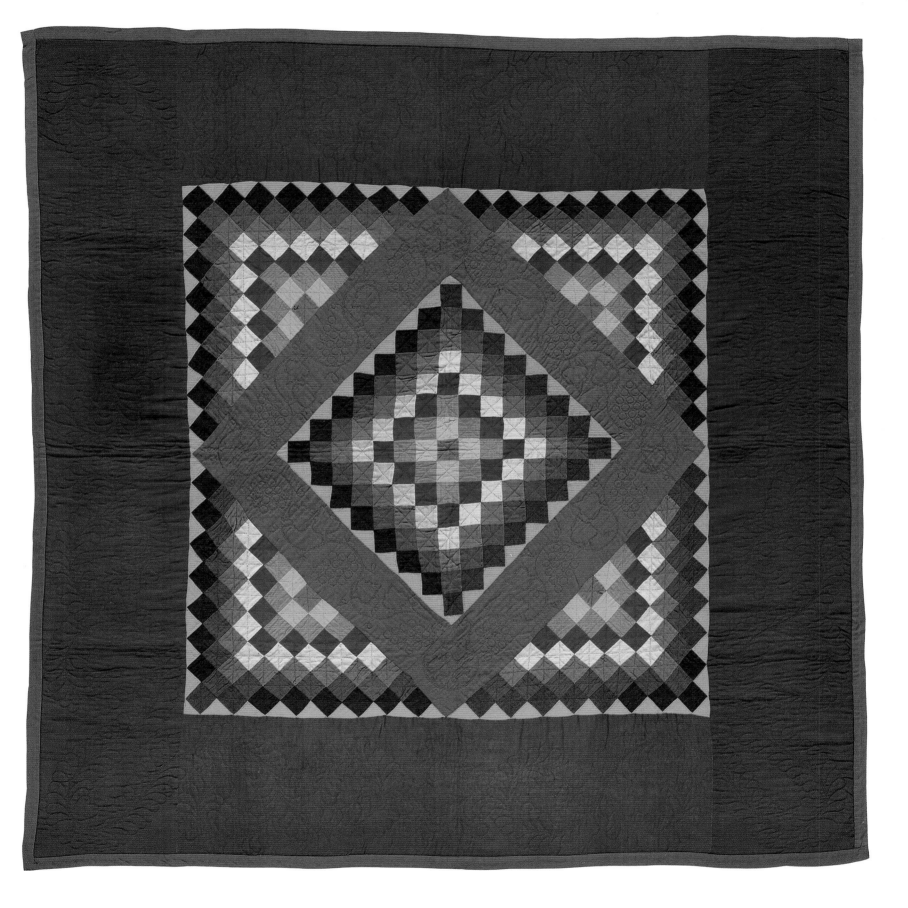

30

Sunshine     and     Shadow

*Unknown Amish quiltmaker, American, Lancaster County, Pennsylvania, Circa 1910, Pieced wools, 80 x 80 inches, 585.082*

Sunshine and Shadow is essentially a twentieth-century development in Lancaster design, named for the abstraction
created by the adroit placement of light and dark colors.
The subtle elegance of the colors and the simple framing distinguish this early Sunshine and Shadow. The quiltmaker stitched handsome,
tight "feathers" into the wide border.

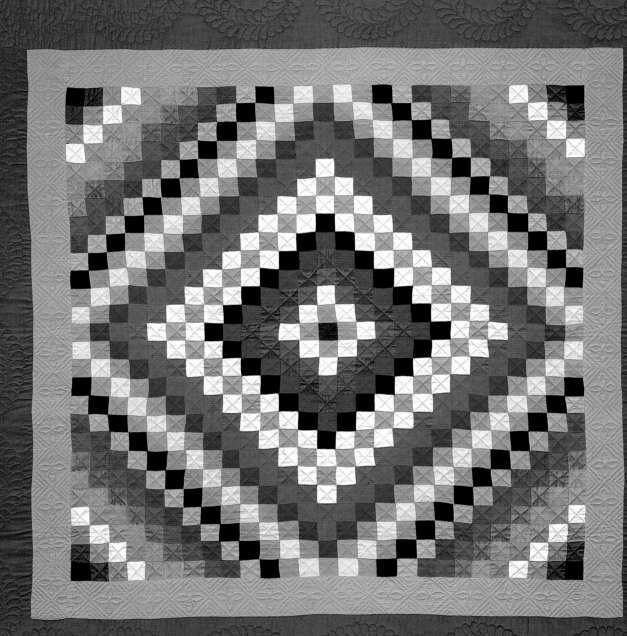

Sunshine and Shadow

*Unknown Amish quiltmaker, American, Lancaster County, Pennsylvania, Circa 1925, Pieced wools, rayons and cottons, 80 x 80 inches, 585.073*

The Lancaster County Amish were a prosperous group; they were also practical and thrifty. Small scraps of dress fabric
were not wasted, they were often incorporated cohesively into the center section of designs such as Sunshine and Shadow. Amish women deliberately
chose the color of their quilting thread to blend with the color of the cloth. Non-contrasting stitching lends the quilts an embossed,
reticent quality, compatible with humility, a cornerstone of Amish life.

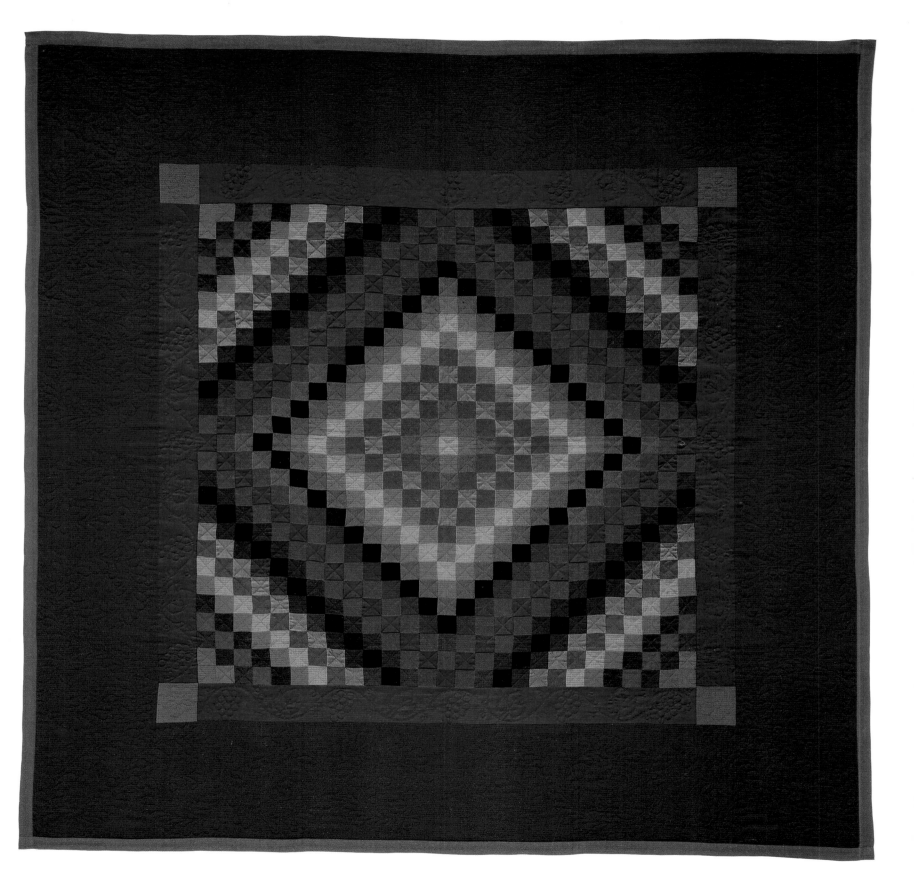

## S u n s h i n e   a n d   S h a d o w

*Unknown Amish quiltmaker, American, Lancaster County, Pennsylvania, Circa 1930, Pieced wools, 80 x 81 inches, 585.067*

Most Amish Sunshine and Shadow quilts were made between 1920 and 1960 and were a more recent development in Lancaster design.
It can be seen as a complication of the basic Diamond. Notice here how the Diamond form is heightened as the quiltmaker "sandwiches" her colors in
groups of three. It is typical to see black used as an accent, rather than a predominant color, in Lancaster County Amish quilts.

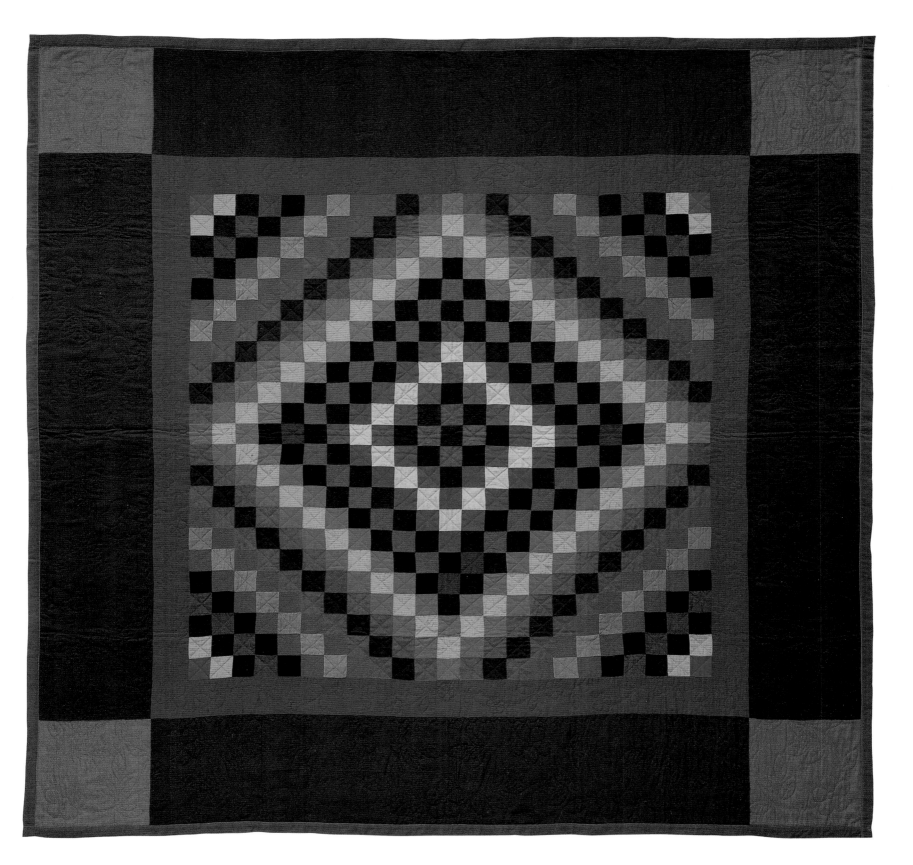

33

# Sunshine and Shadow

*Unknown Amish quiltmaker, American, Lancaster County, Pennsylvania, Circa 1930–40, Pieced wools, cottons and rayons, 79 x 79 inches, 585.003*

Sunshine and Shadow was one of the four or five most commonly made designs in Lancaster.
It offers the quiltmaker exciting possibilities for manipulating color. This example has lots of contrast; compare it with the Sunshine and Shadow
in Plate 38 to see how two quiltmakers' different personalities emerge.
The center of this piece is slightly diffuse; every other Sunshine and Shadow quilt in our collection has
a distinct piece at the very center, set off by its color.

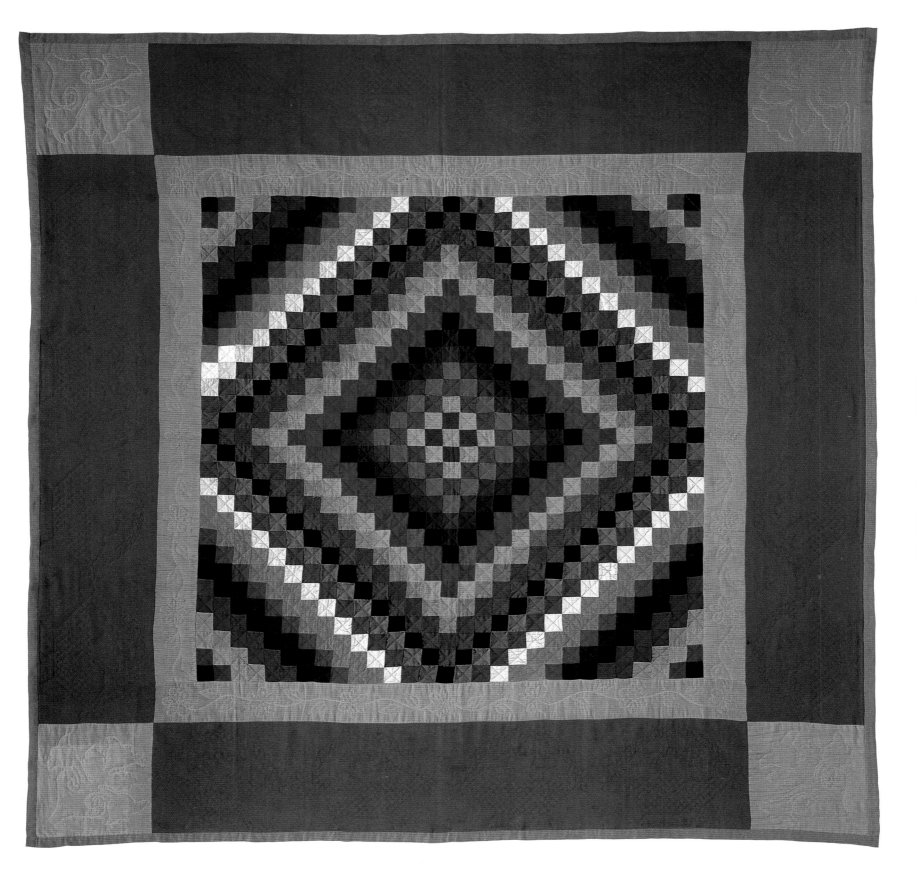

S u n s h i n e   a n d   S h a d o w

*Made by Arie Esh, Amish quiltmaker, American, Lancaster County, Pennsylvania, Circa 1928, Pieced wools, 81 x 81 inches, 585.303*

Arie Esh made this quilt for her son Daniel prior to his wedding in 1928. Though Amish offspring were unlikely to move very far from the family home,
it was traditional for the Amish mother to send each of her many children into their own lives with one or more of her finest quilts.
Quilts made for such special, ritual use are those we are most likely to find still in good condition.

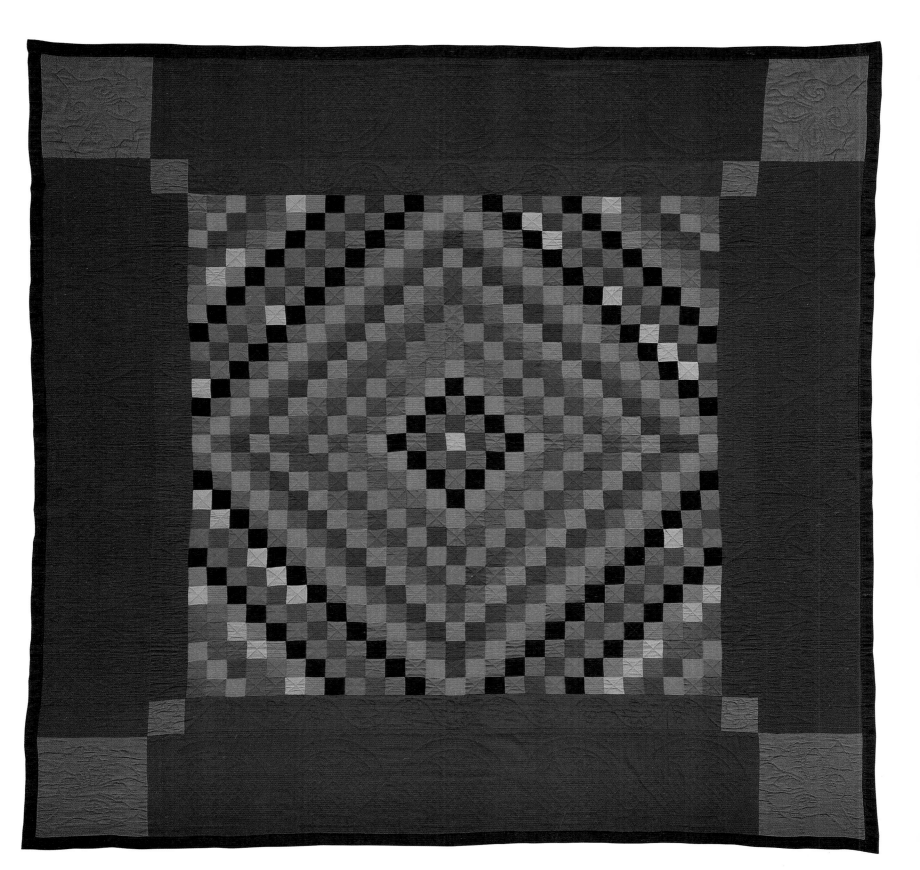

## S u n s h i n e   a n d   S h a d o w

*Unknown Amish quiltmaker, American, Lancaster County, Pennsylvania, Circa 1940, Pieced wools, cottons and rayons, 77 x 79 inches, 585.281*

Seen next to the Diamond, Sunshine and Shadow may seem excessive with its many small pieces.
But between the 1920s and 1940s, when these quilts were being made, non-Amish quiltmakers prided themselves on incorporating hundreds,
even thousands of tiny patches in popular American quilt designs like Grandmother's Flower Garden and Double Wedding Ring.
Relative to contemporary mainstream American quilts, even the most highly pieced Sunshine and Shadow is sparse.

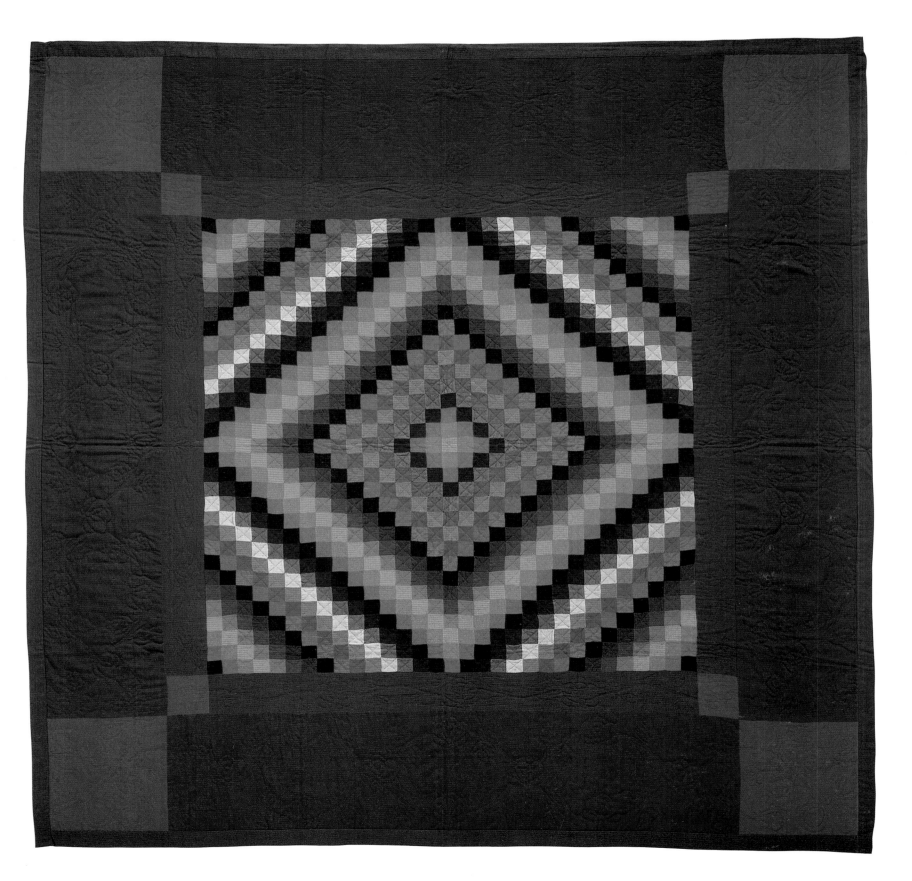

Sunshine and Shadow

*Unknown Amish quiltmaker, American, Lancaster County, Pennsylvania, Circa 1930–40, Pieced wools and rayons, 81 x 81 inches, 585.085*

Lancaster Amish women nearly always piece their quilt tops on the sewing machine. Although most Amish do not use electricity, they are practical people who by the 1870s had brought the treadle sewing machine into their homes, as did the majority of American women. Among the Amish, however, quilting was always done by hand, and Lancaster Amish women were long considered the very finest quilters anywhere.

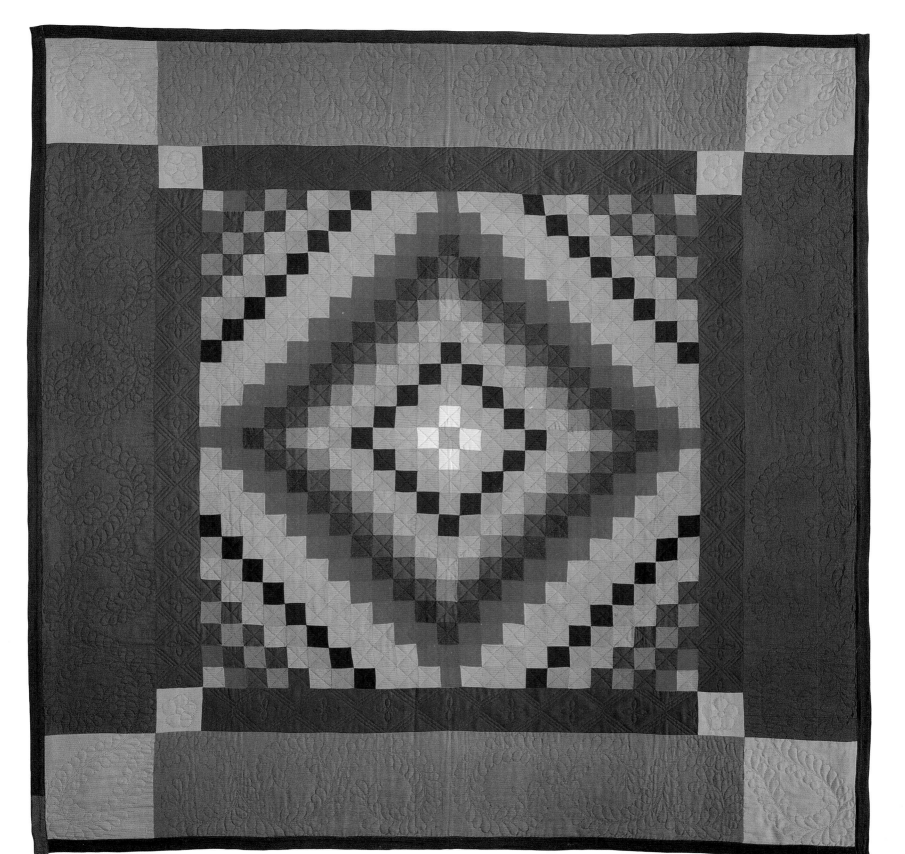

S u n s h i n e   a n d   S h a d o w

*Unknown Amish quiltmaker, American, Lancaster County, Pennsylvania, Circa 1940, Pieced wools, cottons and rayons, 75 x 75 inches, 585.251*

Among the Amish, an individual aesthetic was expressed not in invention but in each woman's decisions regarding design elements:
proportions, colors, fabrics and quilting patterns.
In adding an extra border, an Amish woman could quietly distinguish her quilt. Here, in an otherwise typical layout,
the central design is surrounded by two inner borders, one of them "split."

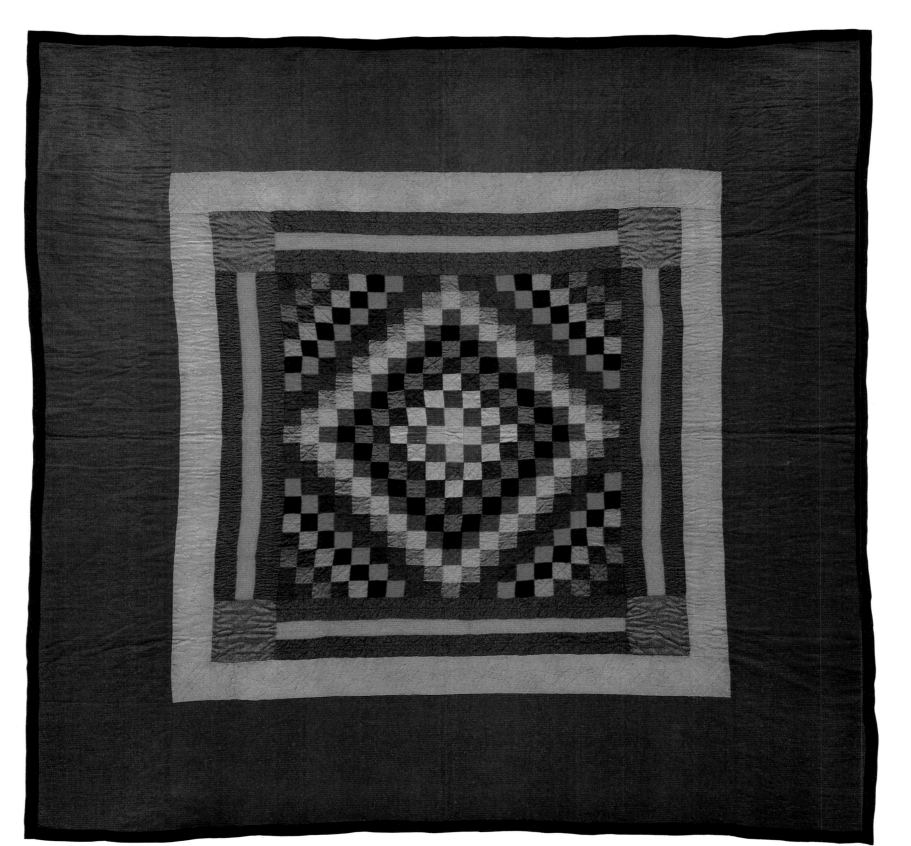

Sunshine and Shadow

*Unknown Amish quiltmaker, American, Lancaster County, Pennsylvania, Circa 1910, Pieced wools, 82 x 82 inches, 585.302*

Among the conservative Lancaster Amish, an individual touch, such as the segmented inner border here,
represents a tolerated but significant break with convention.
Aesthetics is a part of Amish life; in Lancaster it is shaped by a commitment to excellence in workmanship and the highly held values of fellowship and
community. Conformity, in quiltmaking and everywhere else, ensures harmony. There are very few absolutely unique Amish quilts.

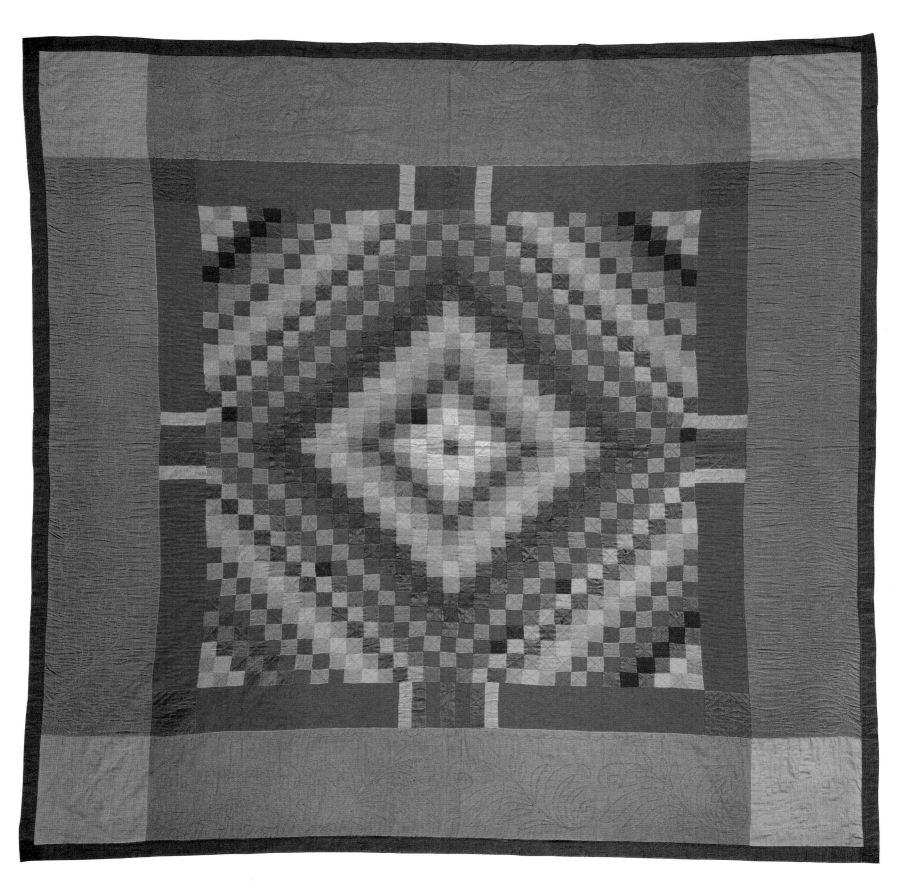

39

## B a r s

*Unknown Amish quiltmaker, American, Lancaster County, Pennsylvania, Circa 1915, Pieced wools, 74 x 80 inches, 585.058*

Lancaster County quilt designs changed little during the classic period (1870–1960), and are more recognizable than those of any other Amish district.
The Bars design is one that appealed most to the Lancaster group.
Nearly as spare in layout as a Bars can be, this one floats within a single wide border. As in many of the great Lancaster quilts,
the stitching is very fine, but being simple and dark, it defers to strong color and form.

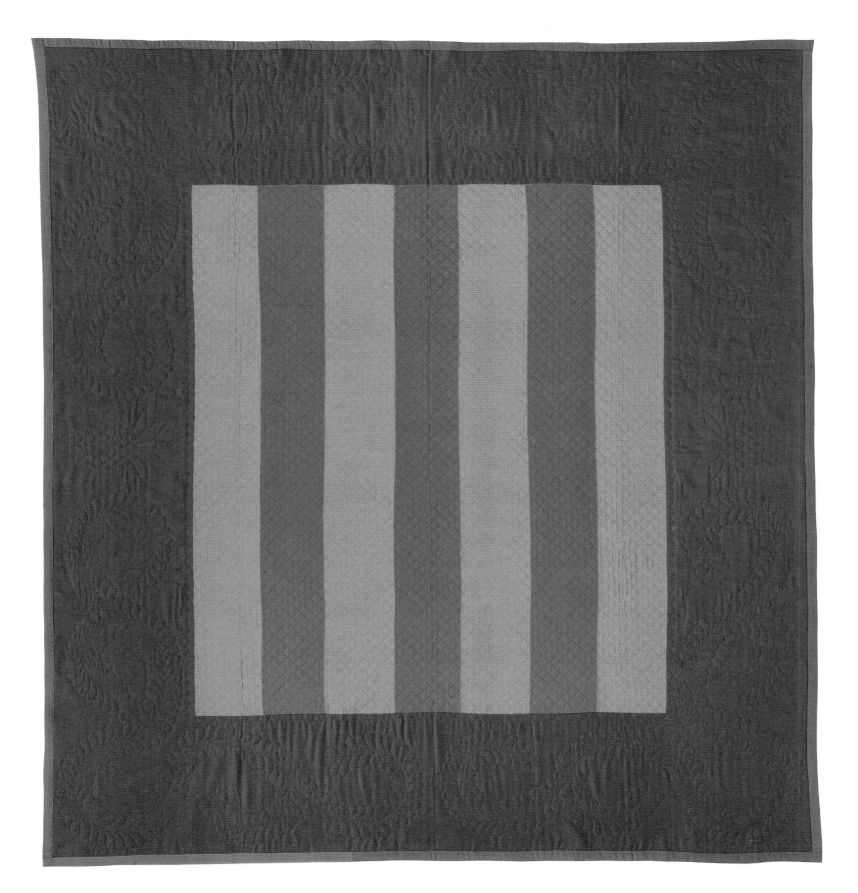

**40**

## B a r s

*Unknown Amish quiltmaker, American, Lancaster County, Pennsylvania, Circa 1910, Pieced wools, 76 x 80 inches, 585.127*

In some of the less well-to-do Amish communities, it was necessary (and for some groups, on principle, preferable)
for the women to use scraps in their quilts. In prosperous Lancaster, we see a fancier, more refined aesthetic with fewer scrap quilts
and a predominance of patterns requiring expanses of fabric.
Look at this piece next to the Bars in the preceding plate (Plate 39) to see what the simple addition of an inner frame does.

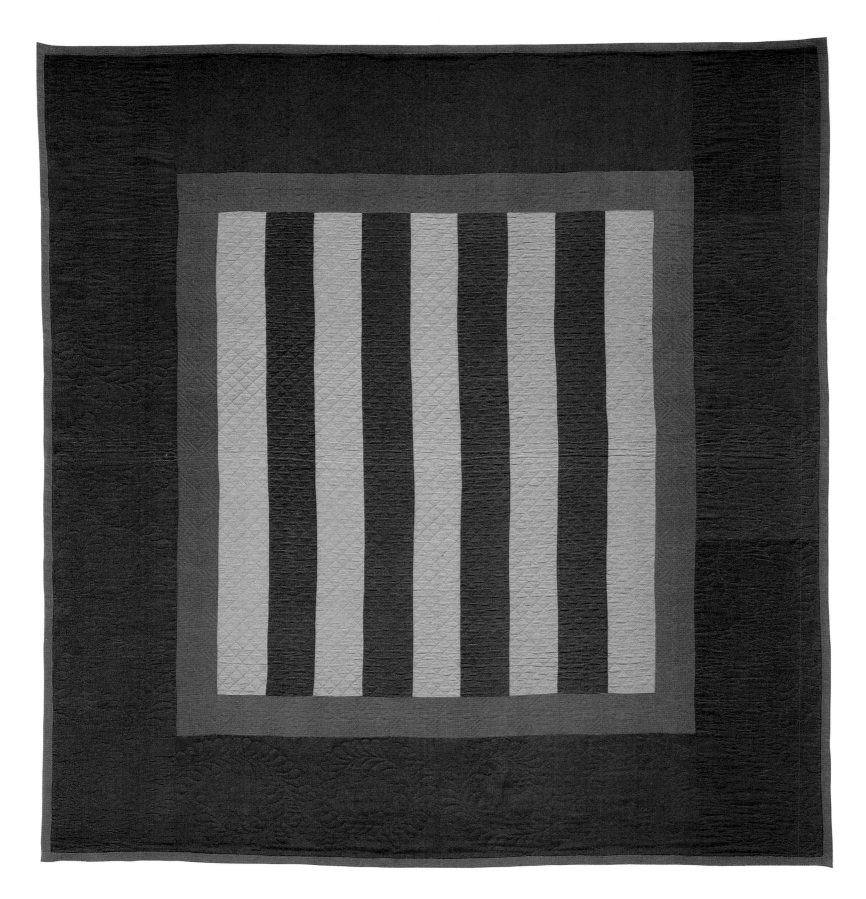

41

## B a r s

*Made by Susan Beiler, Amish quiltmaker, American, Lancaster County, Pennsylvania, Circa 1921, Pieced wools, 70 x 78 inches, 585.191*

This quilt was made by Susan Beiler whose father, "Blue Gate Dan," was said to be one of the first Amish to open the door to tourists.
She embellished the expansive areas of her quilt, especially the wide border, with the consummate quilting for which the Lancaster Amish are known.
Look at what the different placement of "radiant" colors does to the quilts in this plate and the preceding one.

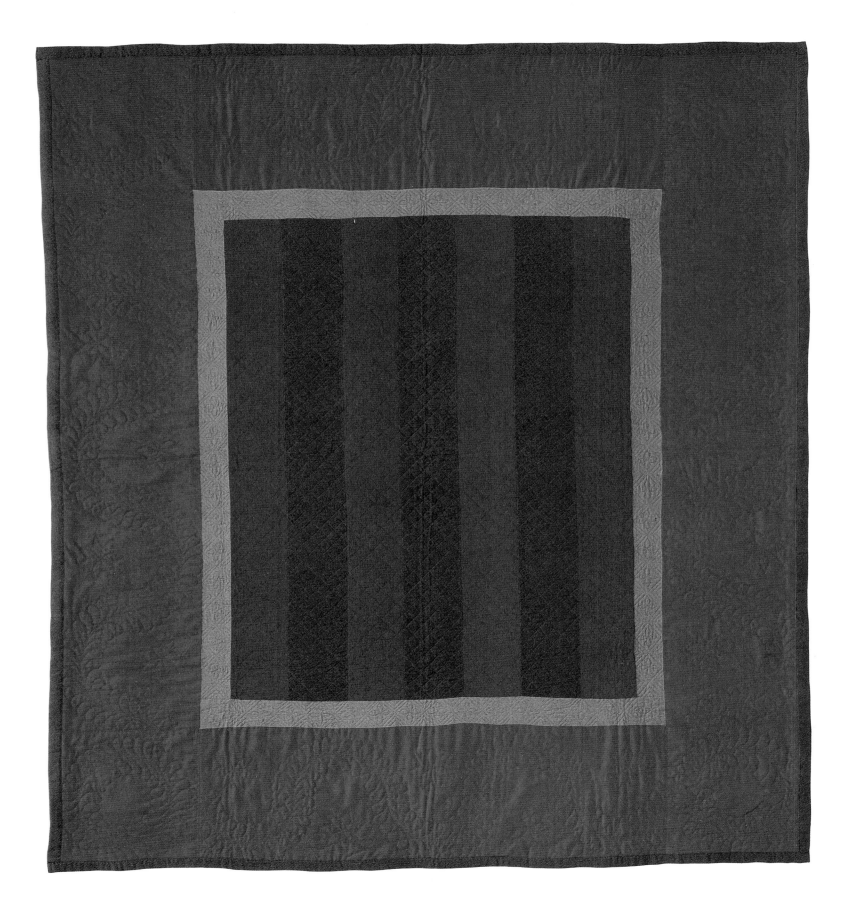

## B a r s

*Made by Katie Lapp, Amish quiltmaker, American, Lancaster County, Pennsylvania, Circa 1935, Pieced wools and rayons, 76 x 83 inches, 585.274*

Our source purchased this quilt in the 1960s from the maker, Katie Lapp, then an elderly woman living in the
mountainous and wooded Honey Brook area of Lancaster County.
Some early Bars quilts have three-sided outer borders (see Plate 56). The inner border here has a minor variation in the purple on one side.
This probably indicates which side Mrs. Lapp wanted at the top of the bed.

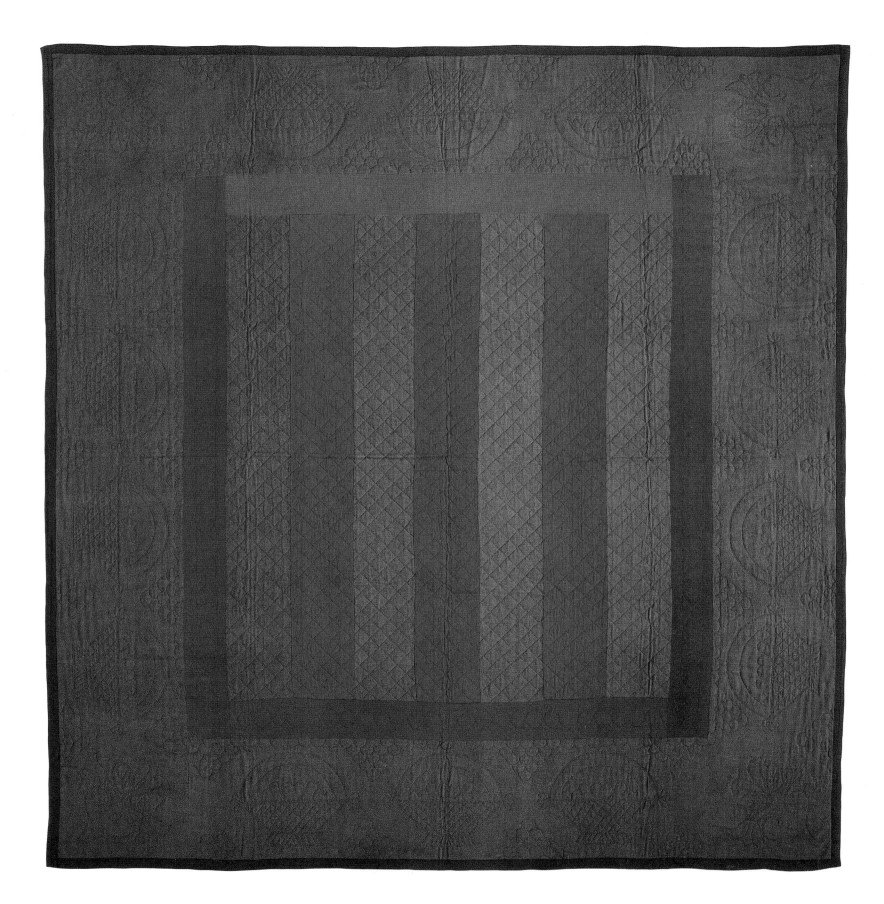

# B a r s

*Unknown Amish quiltmaker, American, Lancaster County, Pennsylvania, Circa 1900, Pieced wools, 80 x 86 inches, 585.278*

Each Amish person strongly identifies as a member of the group. In Lancaster County, then, it is rare to find a quilt signed by its individual maker.
A Lancaster woman might have embroidered initials on the back of her quilt, but these were usually not her own.
Rather, they signify the person for whom the quilt was made.

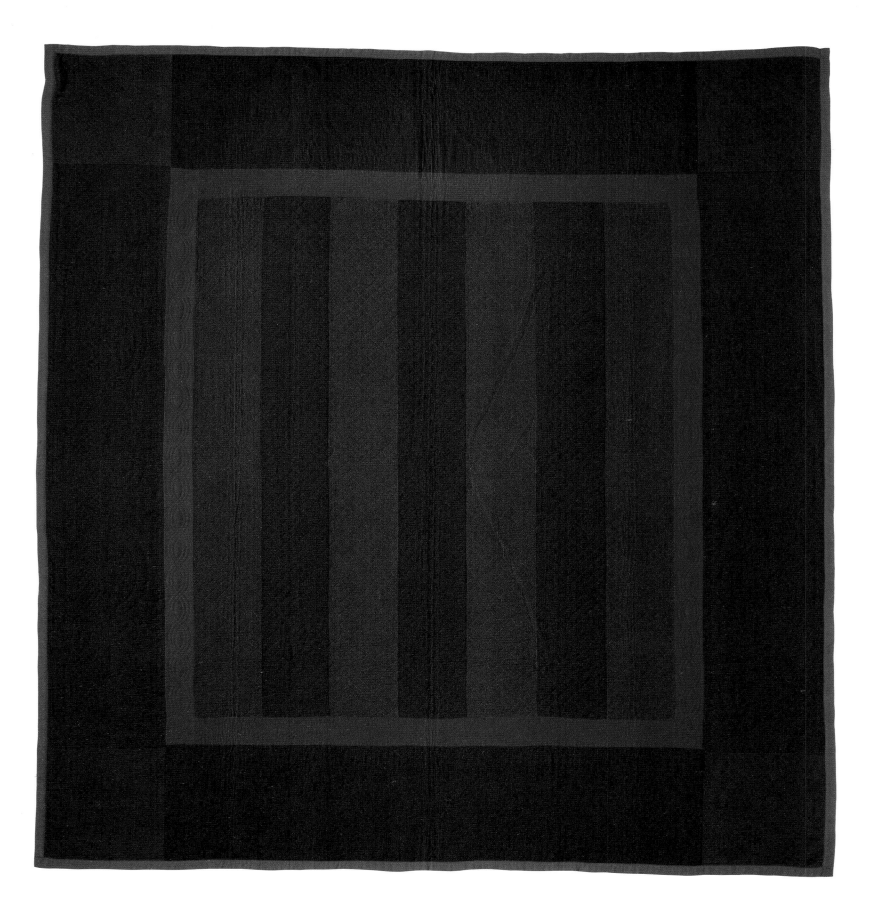

44

### Bars

*Unknown Amish quiltmaker, American, Lancaster County, Pennsylvania, Circa 1940, Pieced wools, 75 x 75 inches, 585.057*

Lancaster quiltmakers often included subtle color changes, which you can miss if you are not looking closely.
Here, the pink and lavender in the inner frame are very close in shade.
Although many all-wool Lancaster quilts are early ones, the simplified, stylized floral quilting and the pastel colors
of this Bars indicate that it is probably a later piece.

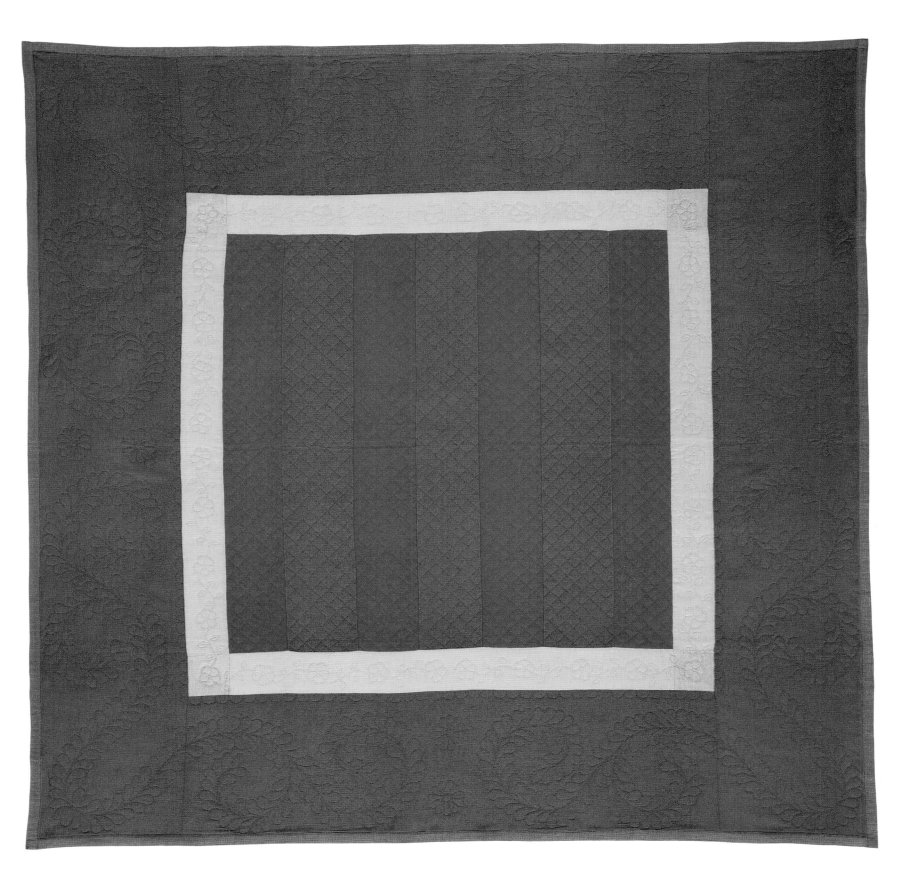

45

## B a r s

*Unknown Amish quiltmaker, American, Lancaster County, Pennsylvania, Circa 1925, Pieced wools, 76 x 84 inches, 585.078*

Printed or figured cloth is considered "worldly" by all Amish groups and is universally eschewed by them. Elaborate quilting, however—
far beyond what is necessary to hold the three layers together—*is* permitted. Plain surfaces take on a quietly patterned look,
with embossed geometric quilting motifs, as well as rather extravagant plumes and flowers.

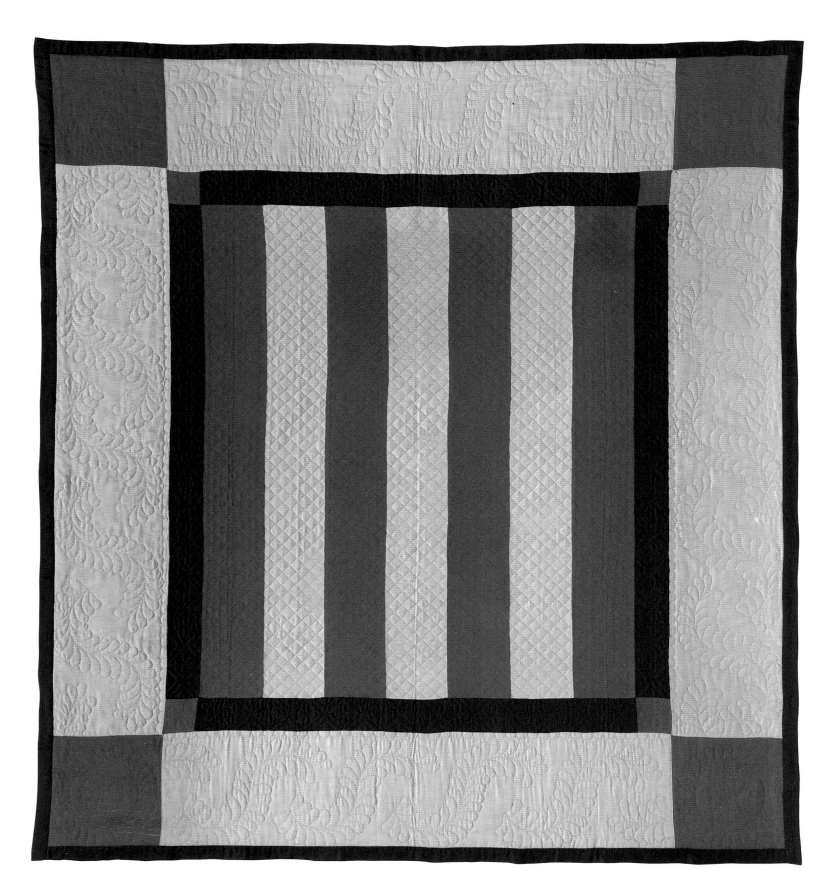

B a r s

*Unknown Amish quiltmaker, American, Lancaster County, Pennsylvania, Circa 1920, Pieced wools, 74 x 82 inches, 585.004*

Quilting, those stitches that hold the three layers together, is an important design element in Lancaster quilts. The flowing
"feathers" quilted in the wide border balance out the angular lines of the piecework and of the "soda cracker," or "waffle," quilting in the center.
Lancaster quilts are typically symmetrical and square; most of their preferred patterns fit the shape.
The Bars alone is better accommodated by a rectangular format.

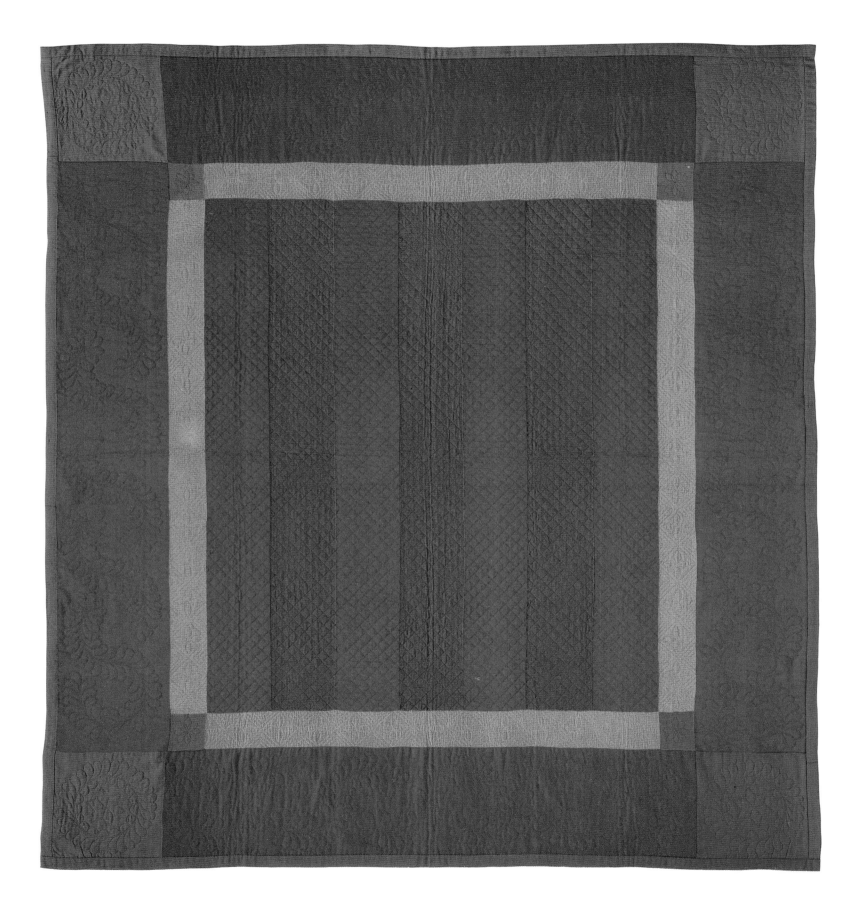

47

## B a r s

Certain geometric elements appear in various forms throughout the Lancaster Amish repertoire; here, diamonds are pieced into the narrow border of a Bars quilt. Although the diamond border shows up regularly on Double Ninepatches (see Plates 67–72), it is not so common in Bars quilts; the Amish family from whom this one was purchased said they had never seen another like it.

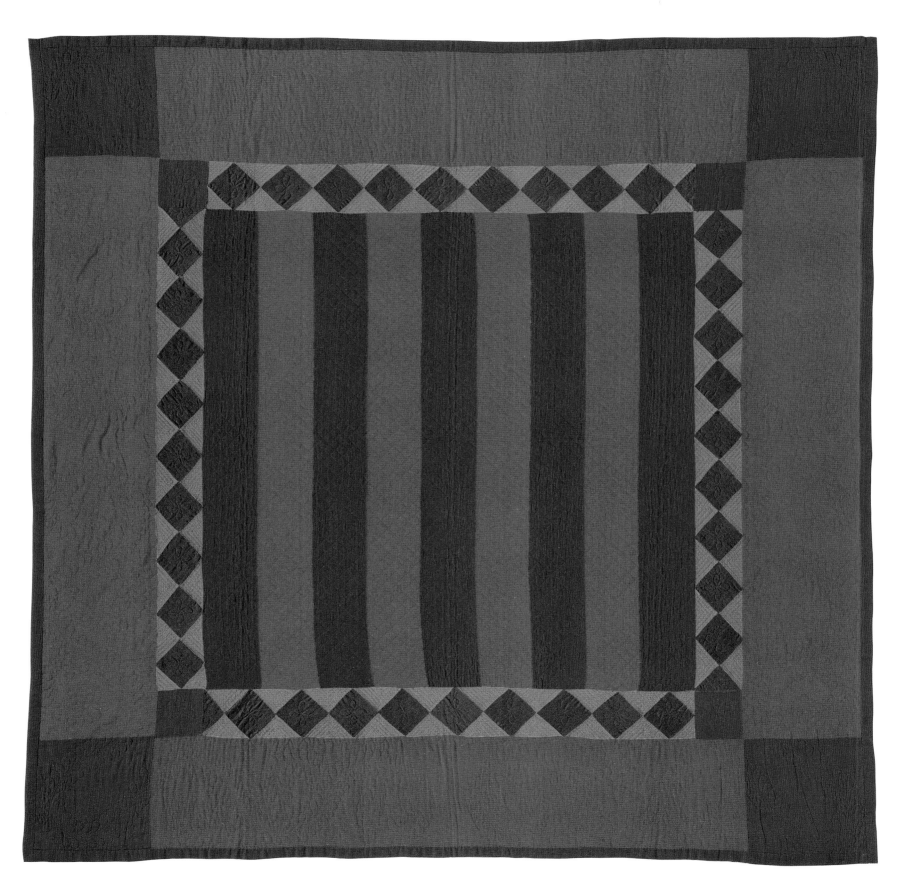

48

**B a r s**

*Unknown Amish quiltmaker, American, Lancaster County, Pennsylvania, Circa 1940, Pieced wools, 81 x 87 inches, 585.295*

Although the Esprit collection was never intended to be a comprehensive or representative sampling of Lancaster quilts,
we do have multiple examples of the designs most frequently made there. We are very fortunate to have had so many Diamond, Bars,
Sunshine and Shadow and Ninepatch quilts over the years to study, compare and enjoy.

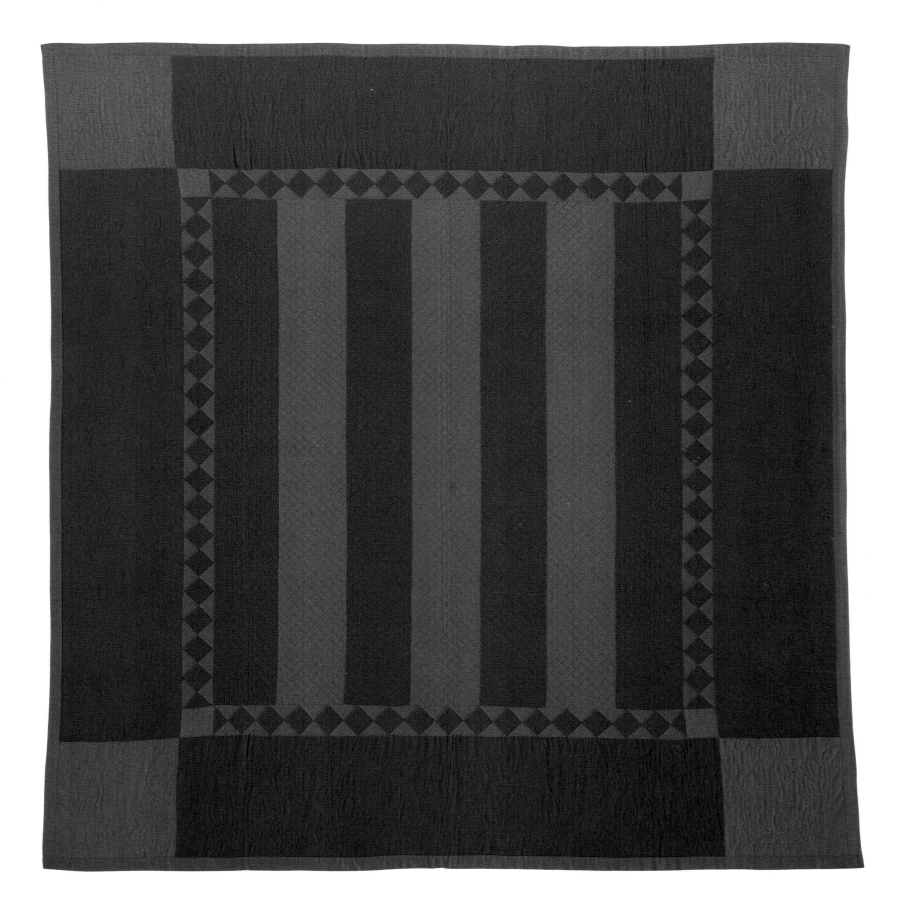

49

## B a r s

*Unknown Amish quiltmaker, American, Lancaster County, Pennsylvania, Circa 1930, Pieced wools, 76 x 81 inches, 585.195*

The basic Lancaster Amish Bars pattern has seven inner stripes. In this variation, known as Split Bars, every other strip is divided into three sections. While this particular modification is seen less often than the simple Bars, it is not rare. For others in this collection, see Plates 50, 51, 52 and 53.

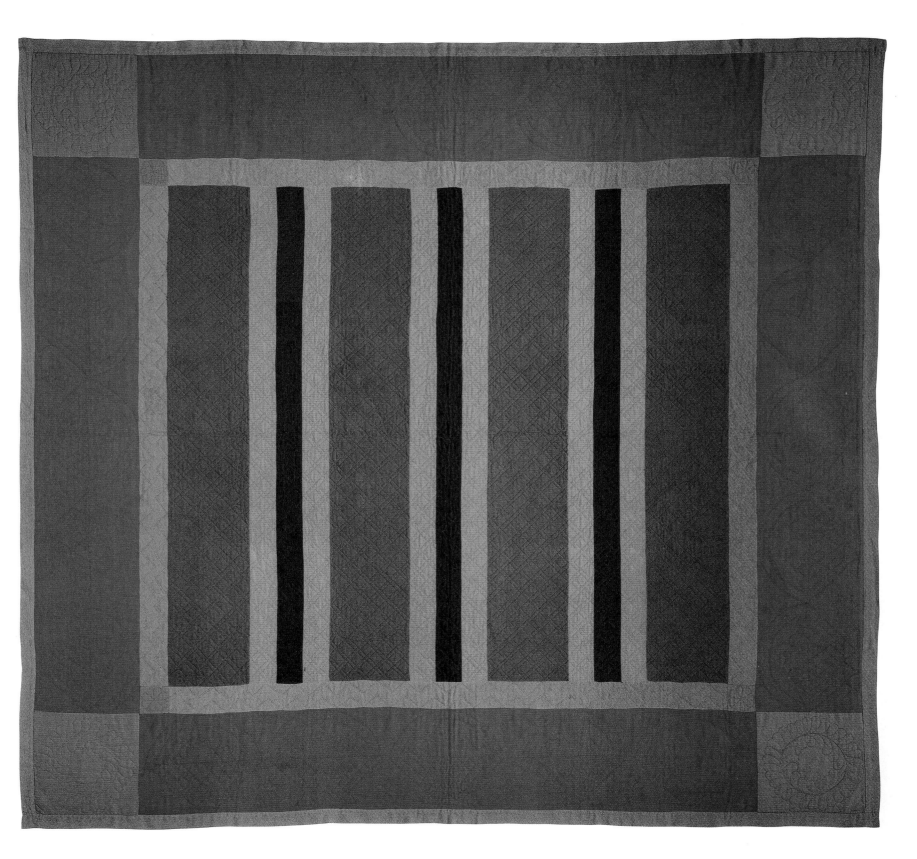

# B a r s

*Unknown Amish quiltmaker, American, Lancaster County, Pennsylvania, Circa 1910–20, Pieced wools, 79 x 81 inches, 585.028*

Proficient farmers working the rich soils of Pennsylvania, the Lancaster County Amish were relatively well-to-do. The women were able to purchase superior materials with which to make quilts and clothing for their families. Fine wool twill cashmeres or plain-weave wool batistes were far and away the fabrics most favored by Lancaster women in their quilts until around 1940. (Granick, *The Amish Quilt*, 78.)

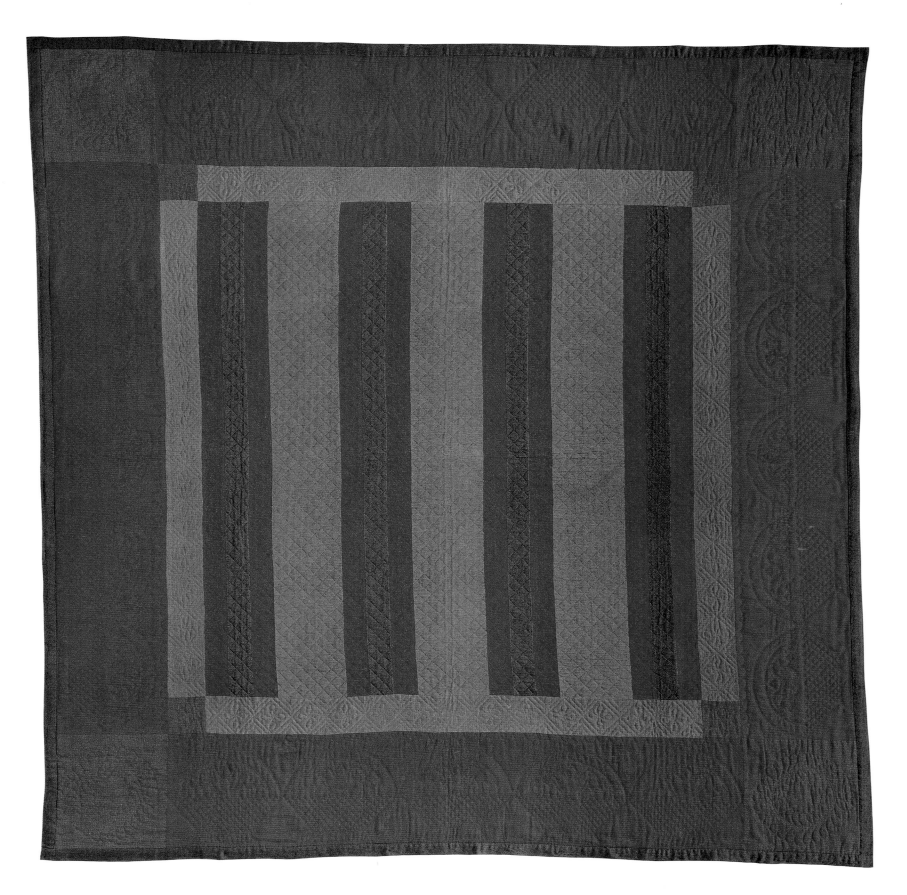

## B a r s

*Unknown Amish quiltmaker, American, Lancaster County, Pennsylvania, Circa 1940, Pieced wools, 79 x 87 inches, 585.035*

Stitched flowers and vines climb the green stripe in this Split Bars, the quilting a delicate counterpoint to the hard, angular lines of the piecework. Amish women sometimes worked almost inconspicuous changes of color into their quilts, using slightly different shades, as with the reds here.

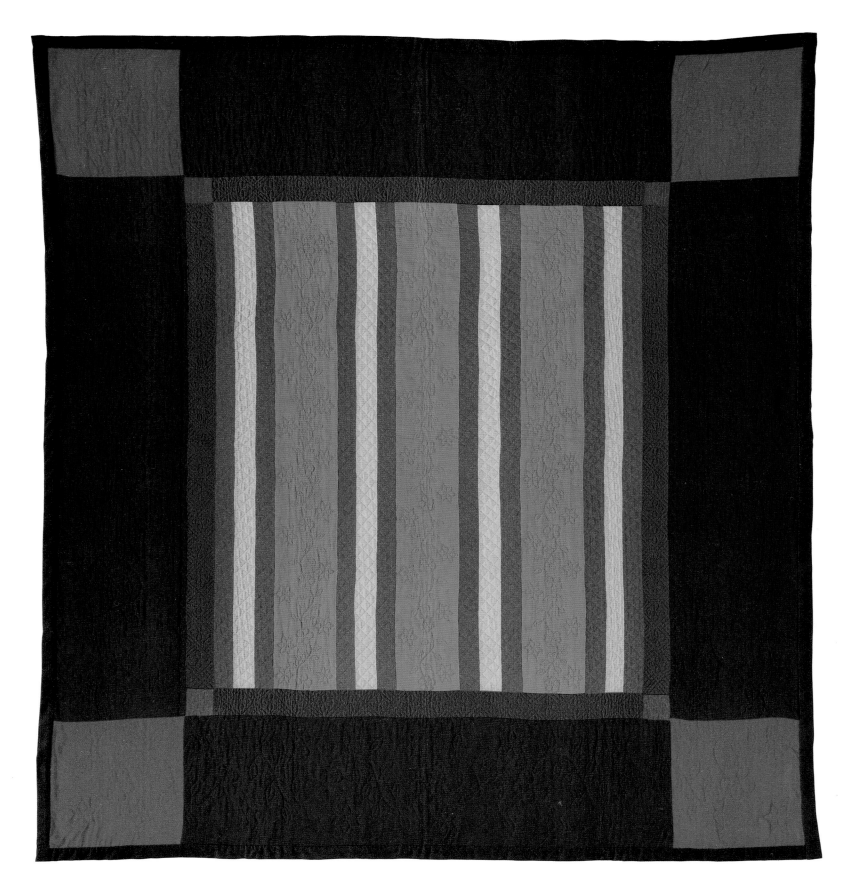

52

B a r s

*Unknown Amish quiltmaker, American, Lancaster County, Pennsylvania, Circa 1930, Pieced wools, 78 x 80 inches, 585.198*

The narrow inner frame here is also divided, echoing the Split Bars in the middle section and creating yet another variation on the basic Bars pattern.
The quiltmaker used red to lend balance and move the eye from the central Bars design to the corners and, finally,
to the wide binding that strongly defines the edge of the quilt.

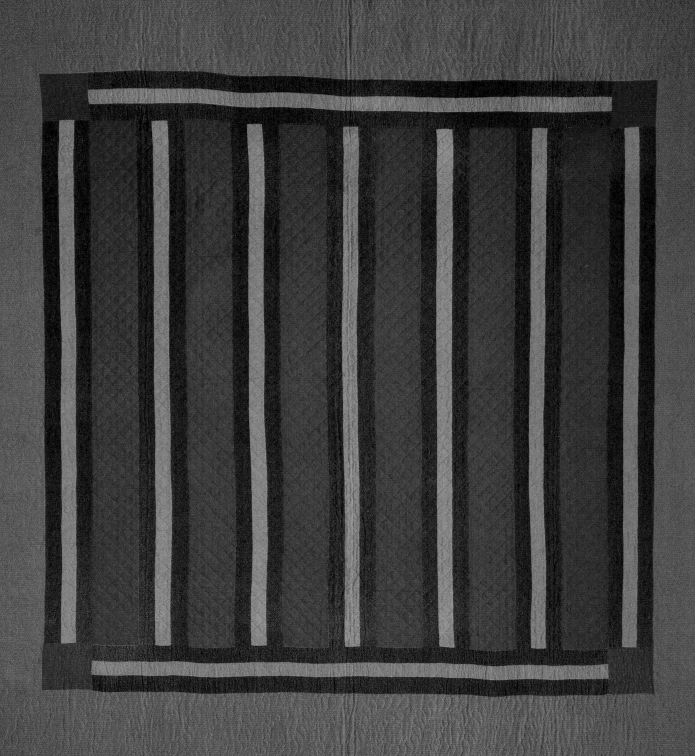

53

### B a r s

*Unknown Amish quiltmaker, American, Lancaster County, Pennsylvania, Circa 1920–30, Pieced wools, 76 x 76 inches, 585.299*

Most Bars quilts are composed of three, four or five colors. The woman who made this curious piece handled *twelve* colors with great skill. With its many shades and slight asymmetry, this quilt almost has the look of a scrap piece. The unexpected choice and arrangement of colors and values create an odd, pleasing rhythm.

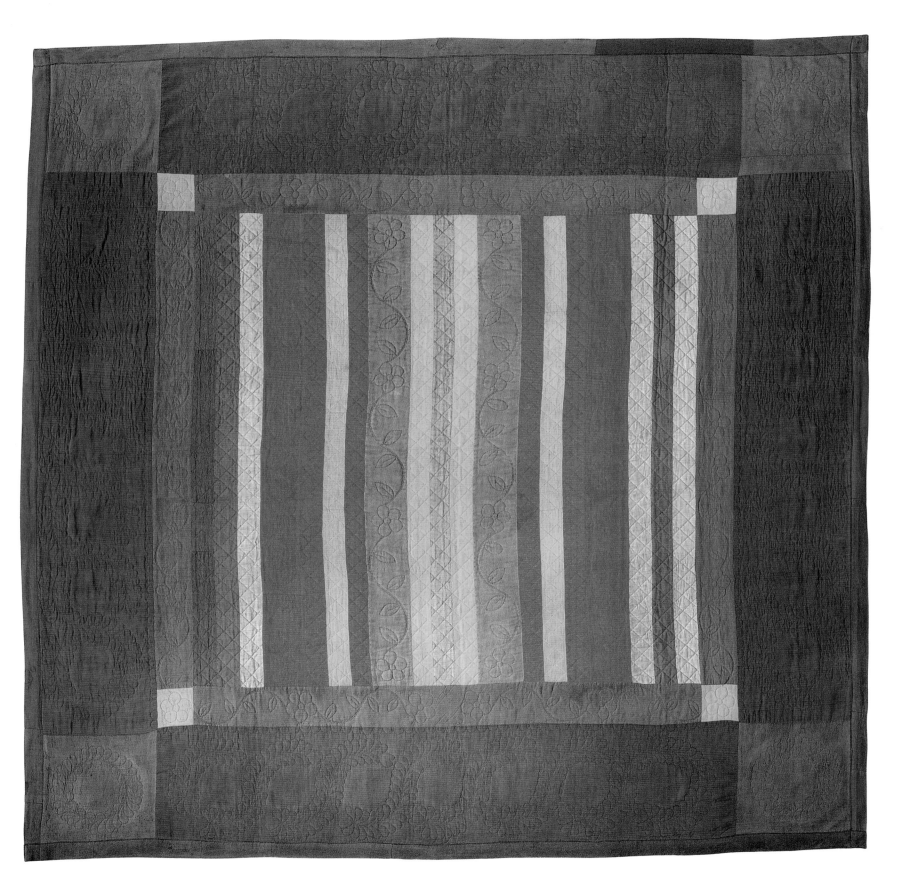

Wild Goose Chase

*Unknown Amish quiltmaker, American, Lancaster County, Pennsylvania, Circa 1900, Pieced wools, 72 x 80 inches, 585.269*

The Amish were not isolated; they lived among their "English" neighbors and were familiar with quilt designs made
by the mainstream culture around them. Wild Goose Chase is a design commonly made by the "English" in Lancaster. But although it can be seen
as a variation of the Bars design, it is rarely made by the Lancaster Amish. This, in fact, is the only one we have seen.

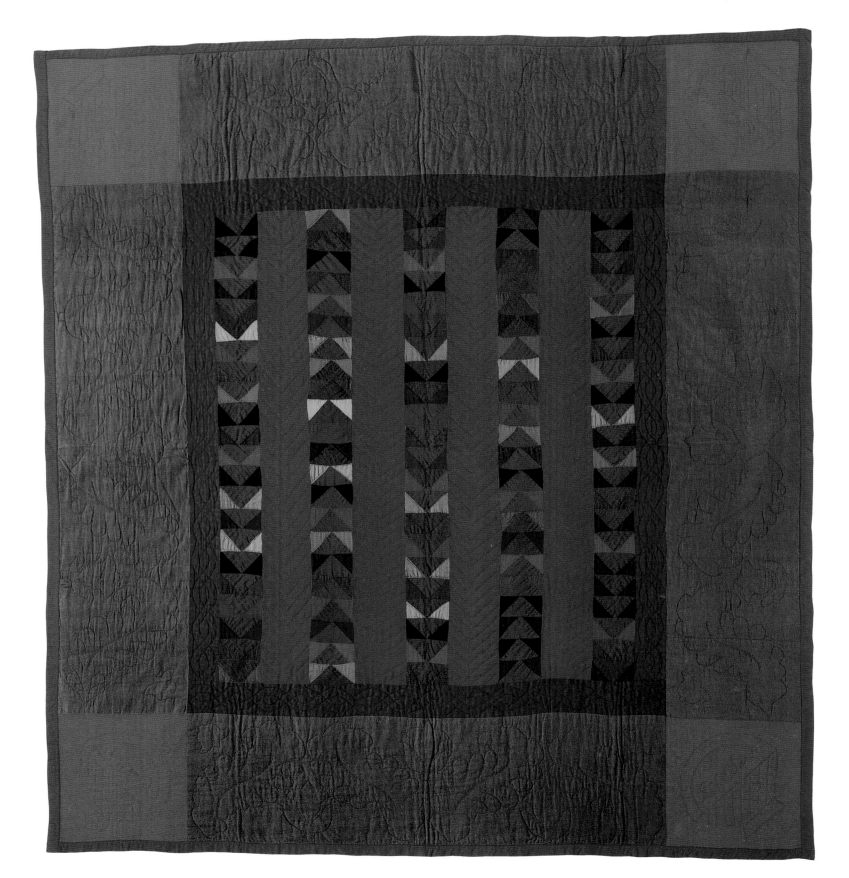

55

## B a r s

*Unknown Amish quiltmaker, American, Lancaster County, Pennsylvania, Circa 1880, Pieced wools, 76 x 86 inches, 585.301*

Few nineteenth-century Lancaster Amish quilts remain, so it is wonderful to see an early Bars. This one, though, has many odd features. The scale and proportions are exceedingly large; the corners are divided in a unique way In place of an inner frame, there is a two-sided border. The quilting is extremely simplified; the clamshell pattern in the outer border resembles the quilting in two other early quilts, Plates 57 and 65.

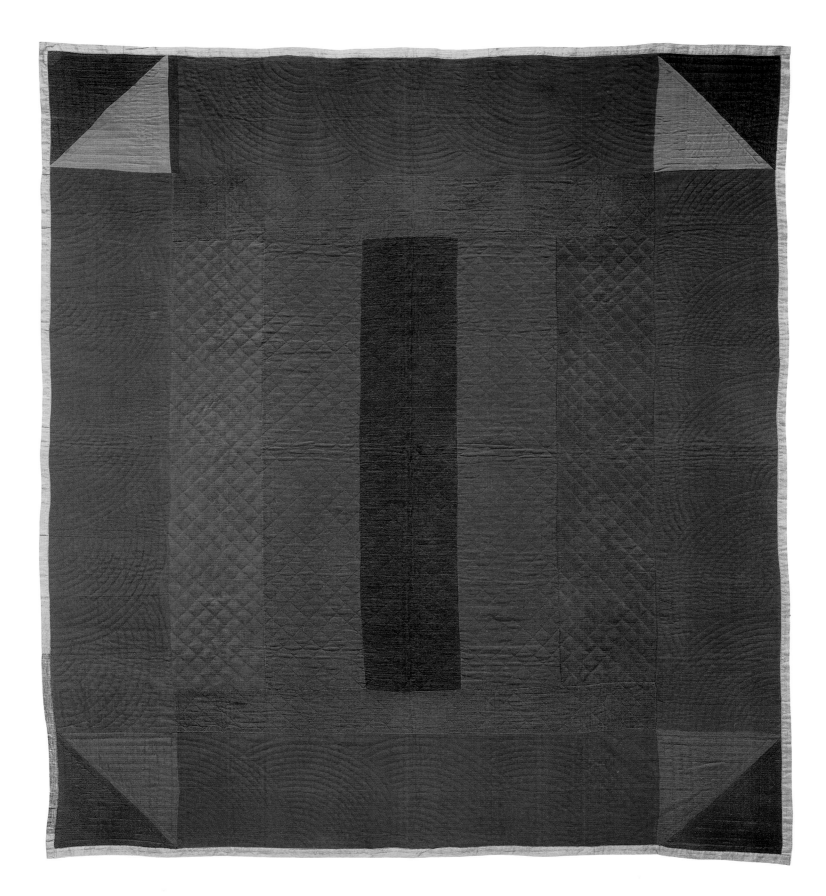

## B a r s
### *Variation*
*Unknown Amish quiltmaker, American, Lancaster County, Pennsylvania, Circa 1910, Pieced wools, 63 x 76 inches, 585.075*

This is the only segmented example of a Bars we have seen. We have wondered if the squares that make up the bars could be swatches,
fabric samples from which Lancaster Amish women ordered wools for their clothing and their quilts. In any case, here we get a good look at which
materials were available to the Amish quiltmaker around the turn of the century.

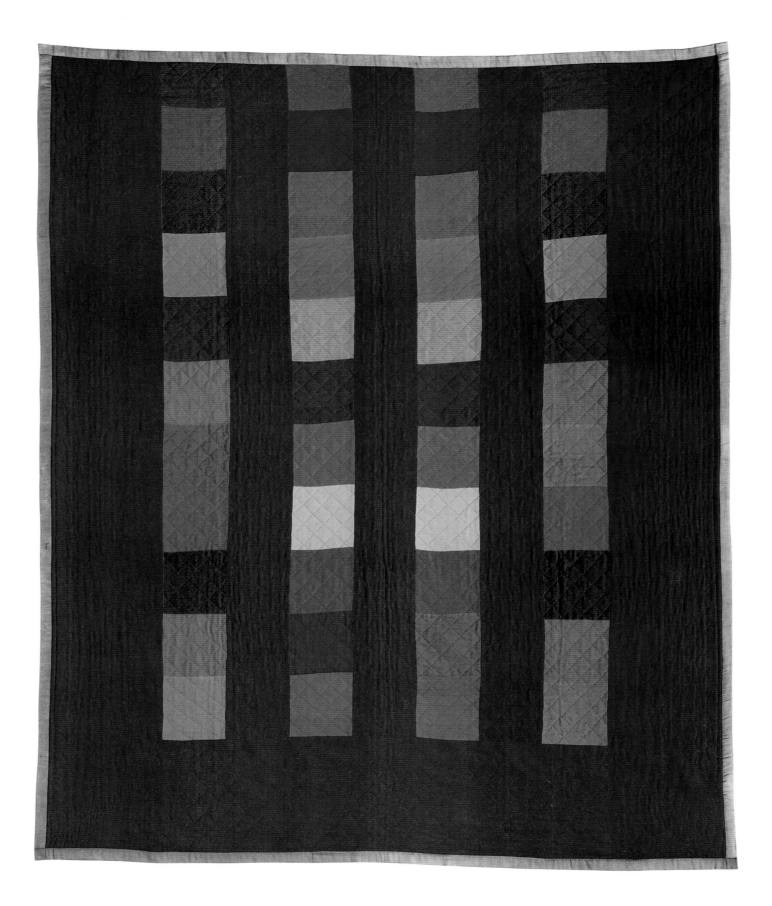

## N i n e p a t c h

*Unknown Amish quiltmaker, American, Lancaster County, Pennsylvania, Circa 1890, Pieced wools, 71 x 83 inches, 585.245*

Perhaps because it is considered a very basic design, Ninepatch is a favorite of Amish quiltmakers. In Lancaster County,
we find interpretations ranging from straightforward and simple, like this early one, to others that are quite intricate (see Plate 62).
Most Lancaster quilts have a variety of defining elements—borders, frames, corners, "sashing" or plain alternate blocks. Not in this early piece.
The patches of rich color run together in this "continuous" Ninepatch, framed by a simple border.

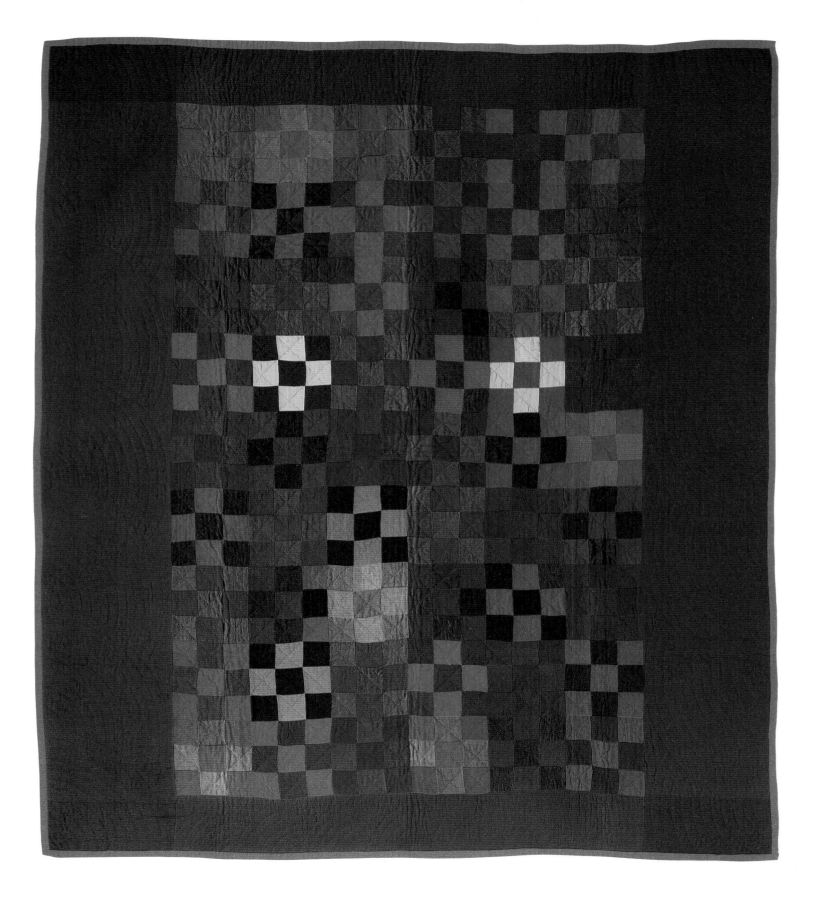

## D o u b l e   N i n e p a t c h
*Variation*

*Unknown Amish quiltmaker, American, Lancaster County, Pennsylvania, Circa 1940, Pieced wools, 79 x 79 inches, 585.166*

Ninepatch is the simple square divided into nine equal parts. It can have many variations. The Double Ninepatch
(large Ninepatch blocks made up of identical though smaller blocks) was very popular with the Lancaster Amish.
This beautifully balanced piece has a constant coral patch in the center of every block. Each small Ninepatch sits within a larger Ninepatch variation
called Puss in the Corner, named for a nineteenth-century children's game.

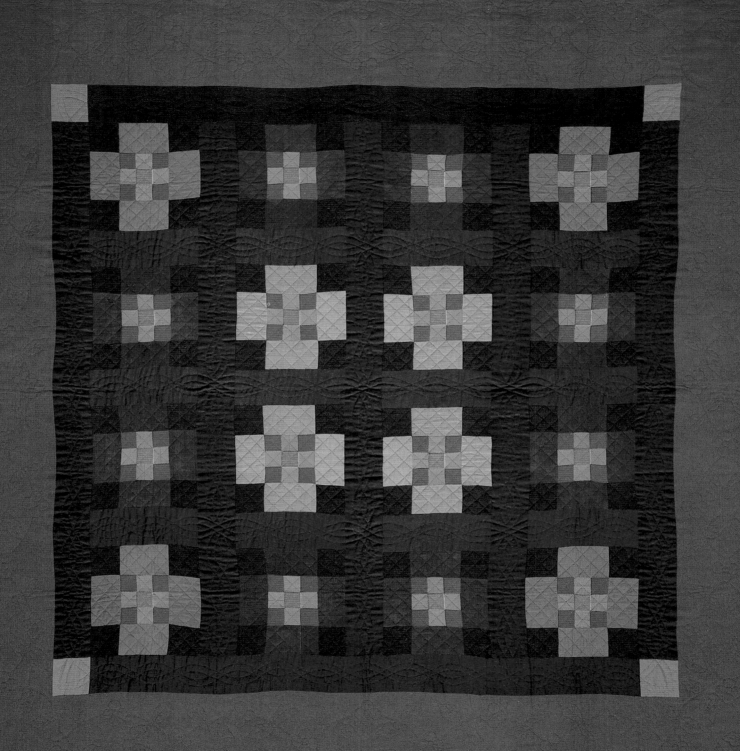

S a m p l e r

*Unknown Amish quiltmaker, member of the Zook family, American, Lancaster County, Pennsylvania, Circa 1940, Pieced wools, 66 x 74 inches, 585.202*

Geometric motifs—diamonds, ninepatches and bars—appear and reappear throughout Lancaster Amish quilts, sometimes as central themes, sometimes as auxiliary elements. Here, the quiltmaker plays with the repeated motifs of ninepatch and bars, large and small. Quilted flowers and vines meander through the center section; we have not seen elsewhere the particular patterns this woman stitched into her outer border.

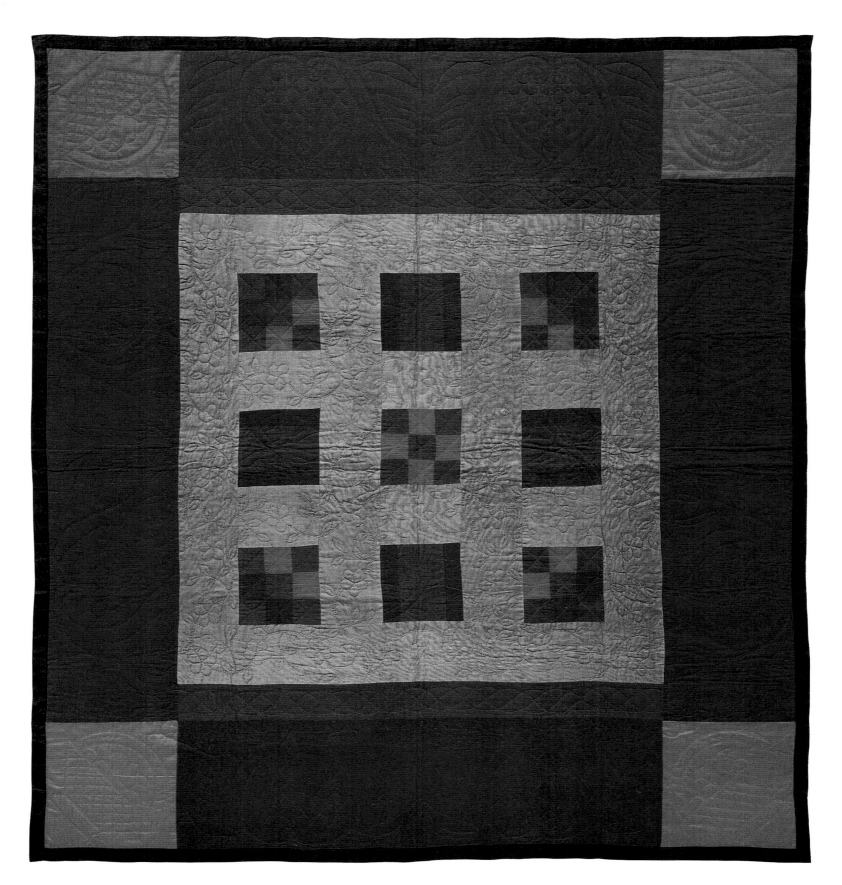

''H'' Quilt

*Unknown Amish quiltmaker, American, Lancaster County, Pennsylvania, Circa 1940–50, Pieced cottons, 78 x 78 inches, 585.300*

Except for this one, patterns based on letters of the alphabet are unknown among the Amish. But such patterns are part of the "English"
quilt vocabulary, in which the letter sometimes represents a family initial, sometimes an organization or concept. "T" quilts, for example, signified an
allegiance with the temperance movement.

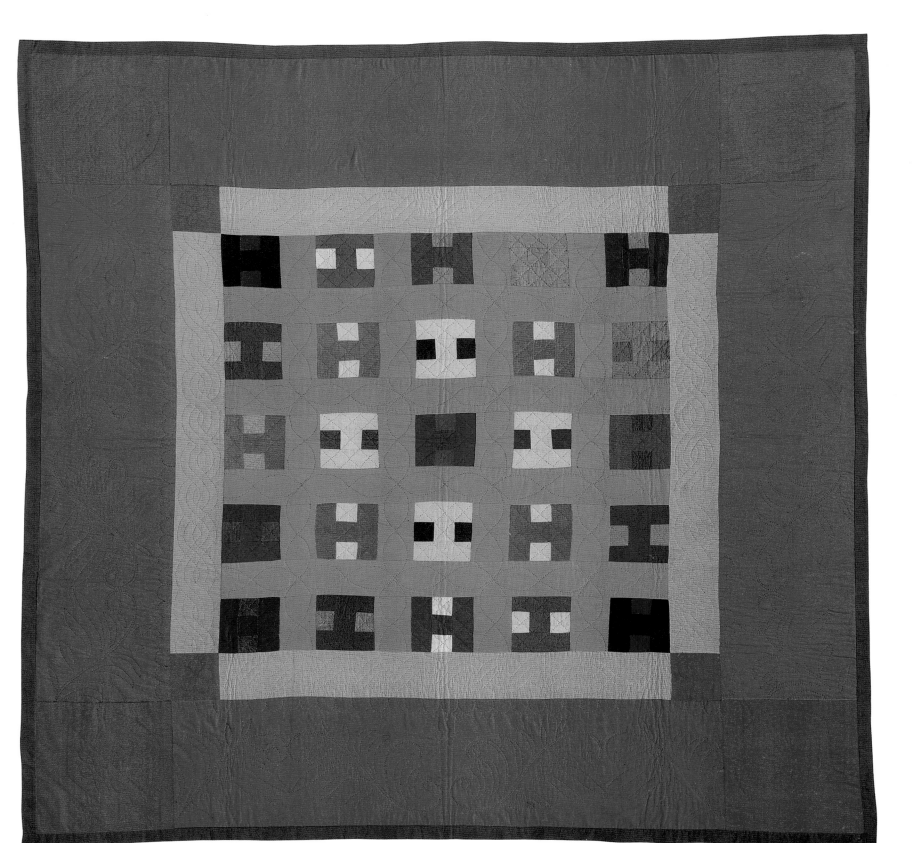

N i n e p a t c h
*Variation*
*Unknown Amish quiltmaker, member of the Zook family, American, Lancaster County, Pennsylvania, Circa 1930,*
*Pieced wools, 80 x 80 inches, 585.158*

Around 1930, a member of the Zook family dreamed up an intricate version of the simple Ninepatch design. The quilt is constructed with all-over repeated blocks, but the quiltmaker used color to create complex secondary designs and to suggest to the eye a center Diamond. The extra Sawtooth border is her unique, personal addition.

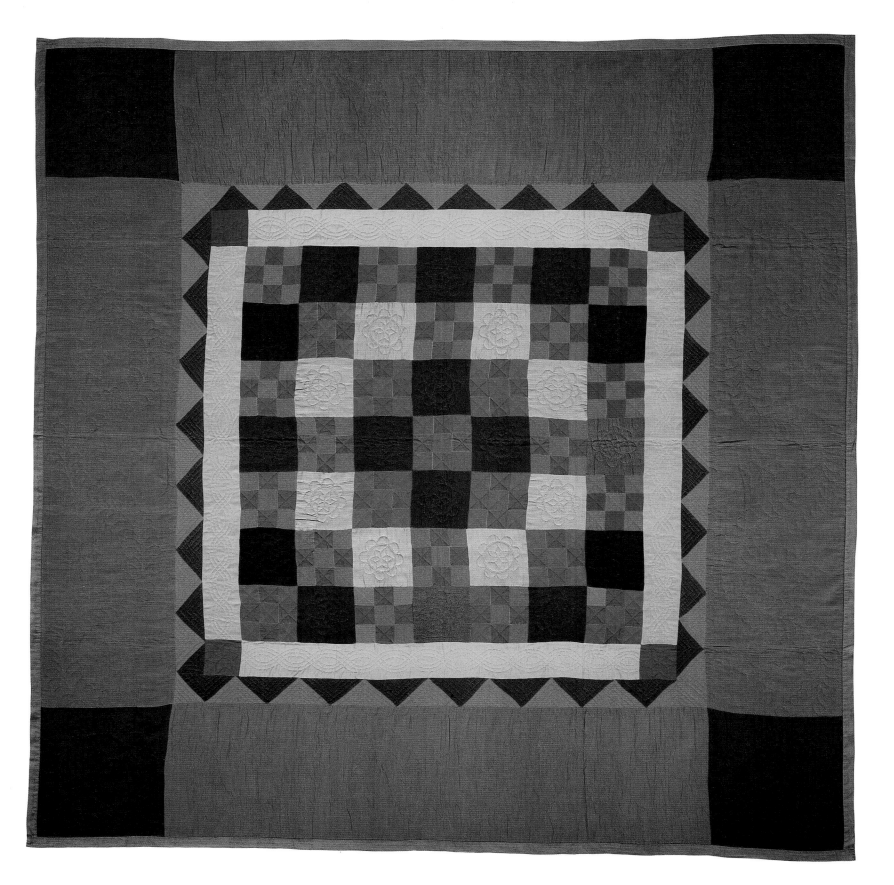

# Double Ninepatch

*Unknown Amish quiltmaker, American, Lancaster County, Pennsylvania, Circa 1910, Pieced wools, 80 x 80 inches, 585.298*

This quilt is a nesting of Ninepatches. Starting with its smallest pieces, it is built of Ninepatches sitting inside Ninepatches,
within a Ninepatch (the whole center section)—all placed in a huge overall Ninepatch. We see it that way because the quiltmaker chose to "set"
her blocks on square rather than on point (as in Plate 67), which accentuates the diamond shape.

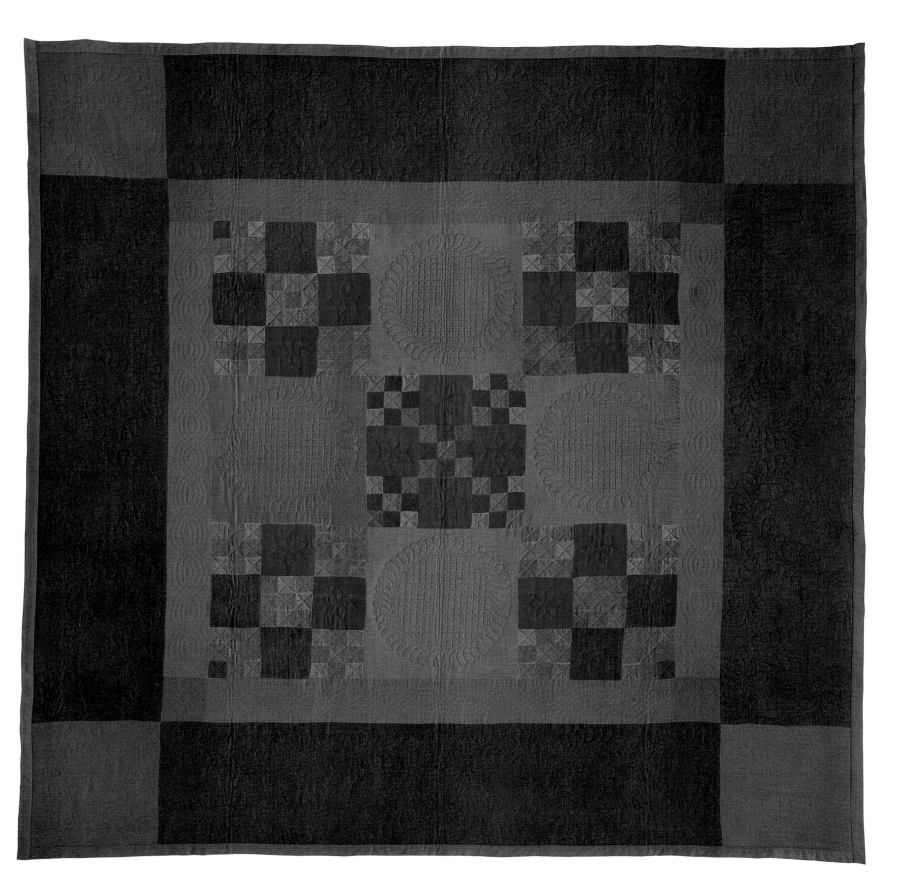

## F o u r p a t c h
*Variation*

*Unknown Amish quiltmaker, American, Lancaster County, Pennsylvania, Circa 1920, Pieced wools, 72 x 74 inches, 585.049*

Though common to other Amish groups (notably those in Mifflin County, Pennsylvania), the Fourpatch is rarely worked in Lancaster. This woman distinguished her quilt in other ways: she manipulated her colors to create the illusion of a central cross in what are actually simple, repeated Fourpatch blocks. The black "gridding" and green inner corners are her own variations on the conventional Lancaster format.

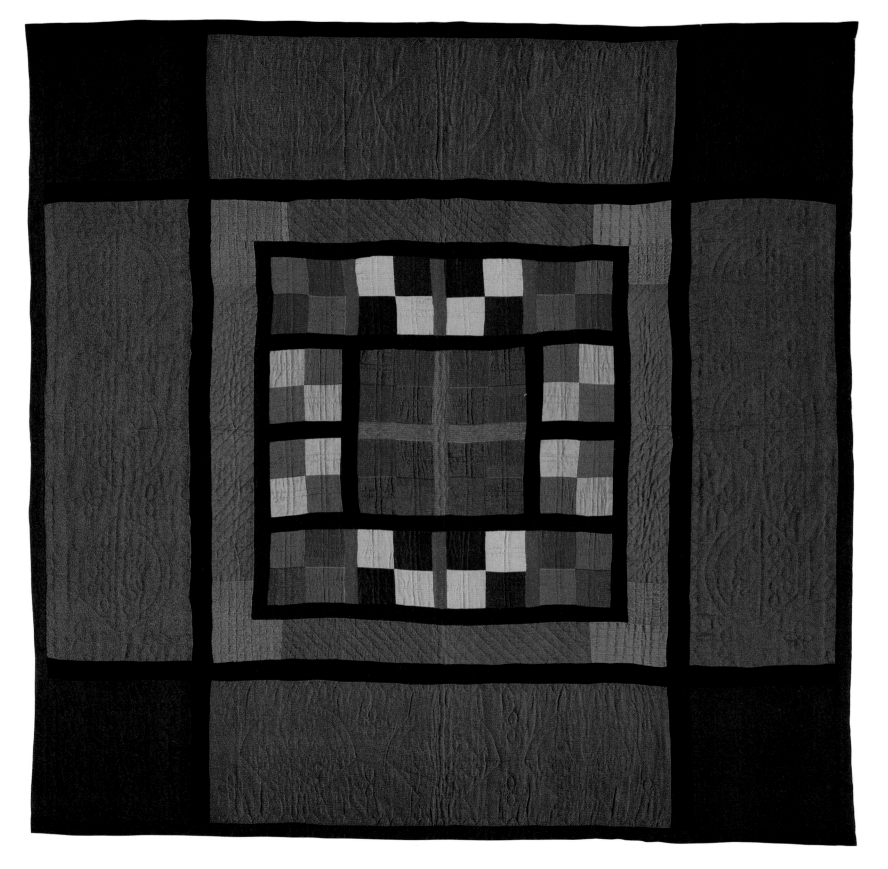

# N i n e p a t c h

*Made by Mary Stoltzfoos, Amish quiltmaker, American, Lancaster County, Pennsylvania, Circa 1920, Pieced wools, rayons, silks and cottons, 75 x 84 inches, 585.263*

Sometimes when we purchase a quilt, we are fortunate in getting information on its origin from our sources
(typically, trusted neighbors of Amish families). This time we were told that the Stoltzfoos family reported that "the quilting
pattern in the border was adapted from some old wallpaper."
Notice again how in this quilt (collected in the Christiana area of Lancaster County) color has been
deliberately organized to create the illusion of a center.

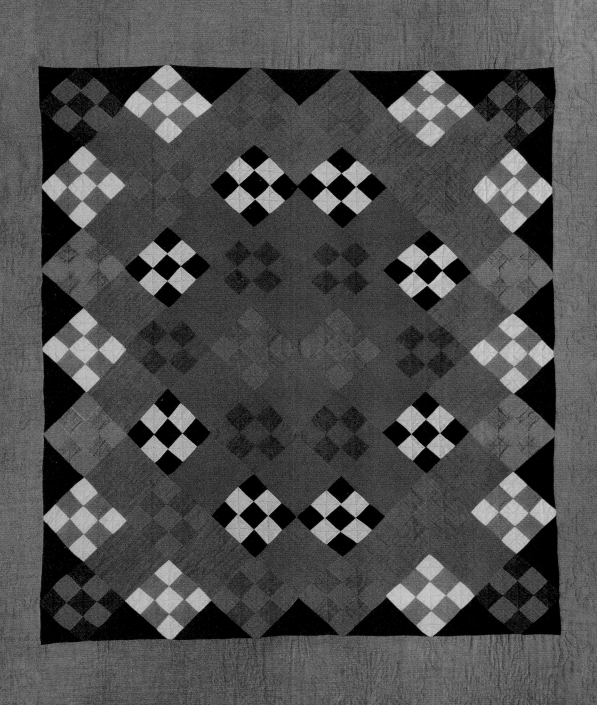

## Ninepatch

*Unknown Amish quiltmaker, American, Lancaster County, Pennsylvania, Circa 1880–90, Pieced wools, 88 x 88 inches, 585.147*

This nineteenth-century piece was made for Mary Blank of Monterey in Lancaster County. The center section gives us a look at
a variety of colors and fabrics used in early Lancaster quilts.
The quilting and the "sashing" of this nineteenth-century Ninepatch are quite different from the later one in the preceding plate. Compare it, too,
with the Basket of Chips in Plate 76.

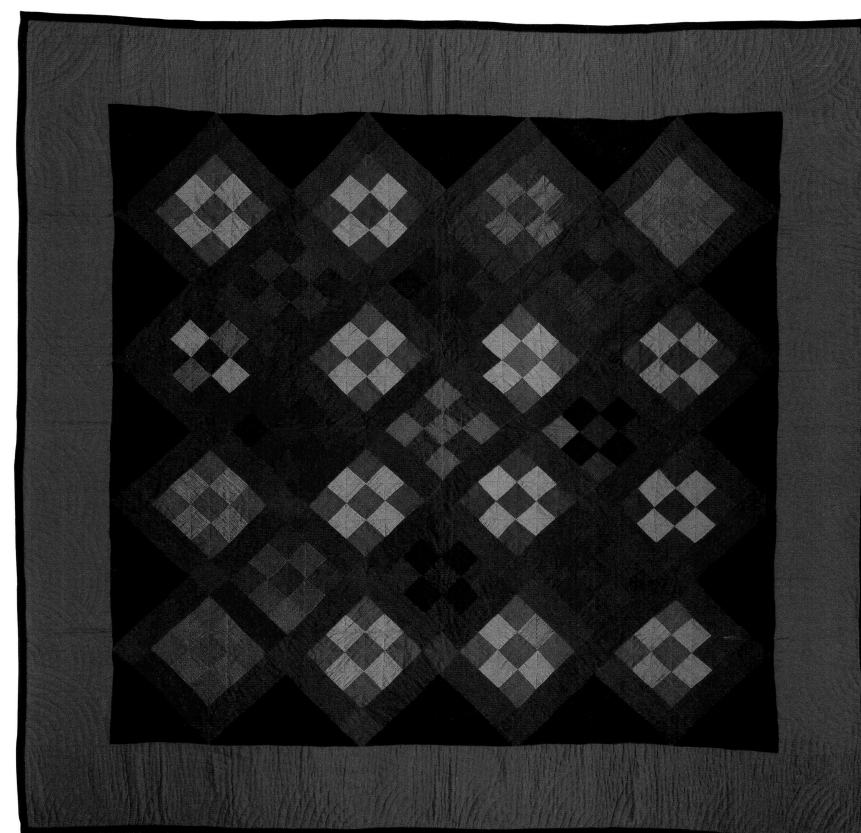

Double Ninepatch

*Unknown Amish quiltmaker, American, Lancaster County, Pennsylvania, Circa 1930–40, Pieced wools and rayons, 72 x 72 inches, 585.012*

Examining this quilt next to one similar in construction (Plate 62), we can see how the final look is affected by the maker's aesthetic decisions. Even the choice of fabrics can make a difference: it is easier to piece and quilt very precisely with the wools of the other quilt than with the synthetic fabrics included in this one. Note the addition here of tiny Ninepatch blocks in the inner corners.

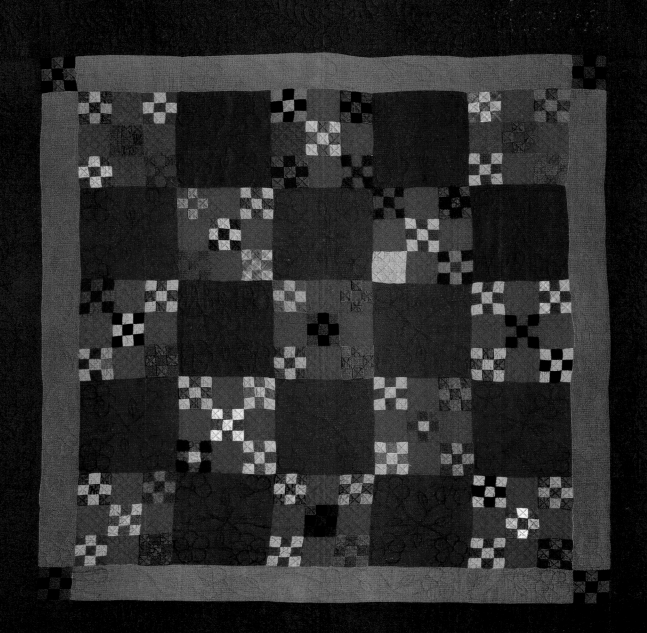

## Double Ninepatch

*Unknown Amish quiltmaker, American, Lancaster County, Pennsylvania, Circa 1919, Pieced wools, 77 x 85 inches, 585.045*

Most of the fine Lancaster County Amish quilts left today were "made special"—either as gifts, for "Sunday" or for special occasions like weddings.
Everyday quilts were much simpler and practical; some were even tied comforters.
This piece was made for Annie Esh before she married John Stoltzfus in 1919. Although we are not certain who made the quilt,
it was probably Annie's mother. The initials "AE" are cross-stitched on a corner of the back.

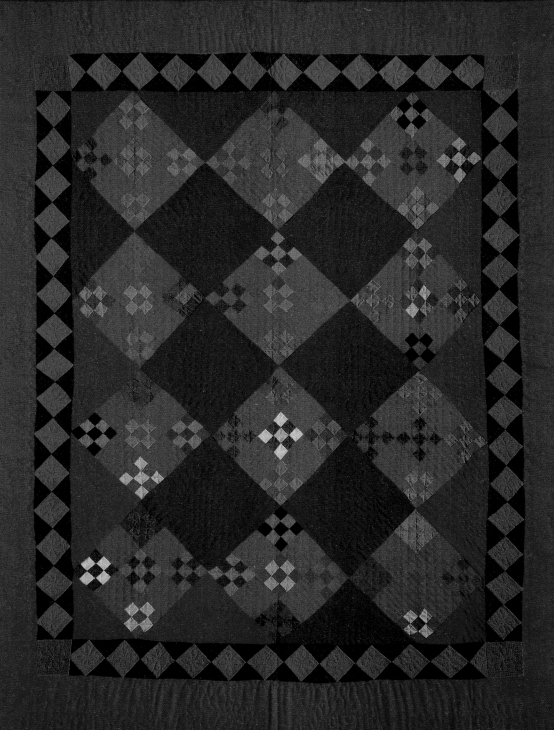

## D o u b l e   N i n e p a t c h

*Unknown Amish quiltmaker, American, Lancaster County, Pennsylvania, Circa 1930, Pieced wools and rayons, 82 x 85 inches, 585.018*

Some Amish women probably welcomed synthetic fabrics; others preferred to work only with natural fibers. At certain points, however,
such as during the war, rayons and nylons were almost the only available materials. Designs like Sunshine and Shadow and Ninepatch which incorporate
many small scraps are likely to combine a variety of natural and man-made fabrics.

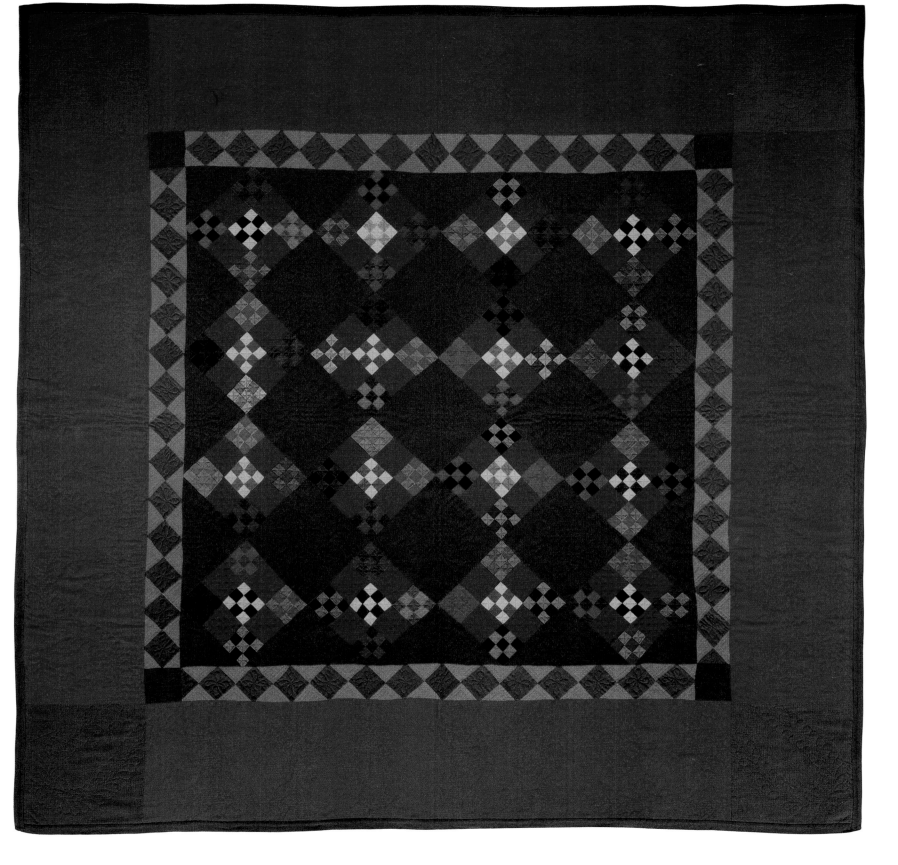

Double Ninepatch

*Dorothy Beiler, Amish quiltmaker, American, Lancaster County, Pennsylvania, Circa 1929, Pieced wools and rayons, 80 x 82 inches, 585.005*

When we got this quilt, we were given the maker's name but, unfortunately, nothing to help explain why Dorothy Beiler included
one light blue diamond in the border. It is rare for a Lancaster quilt to have an "outstanding" piece. Even in quilts using many different colors,
Amish quiltmakers strove for overall balance and harmony rather than calling attention to any one area.

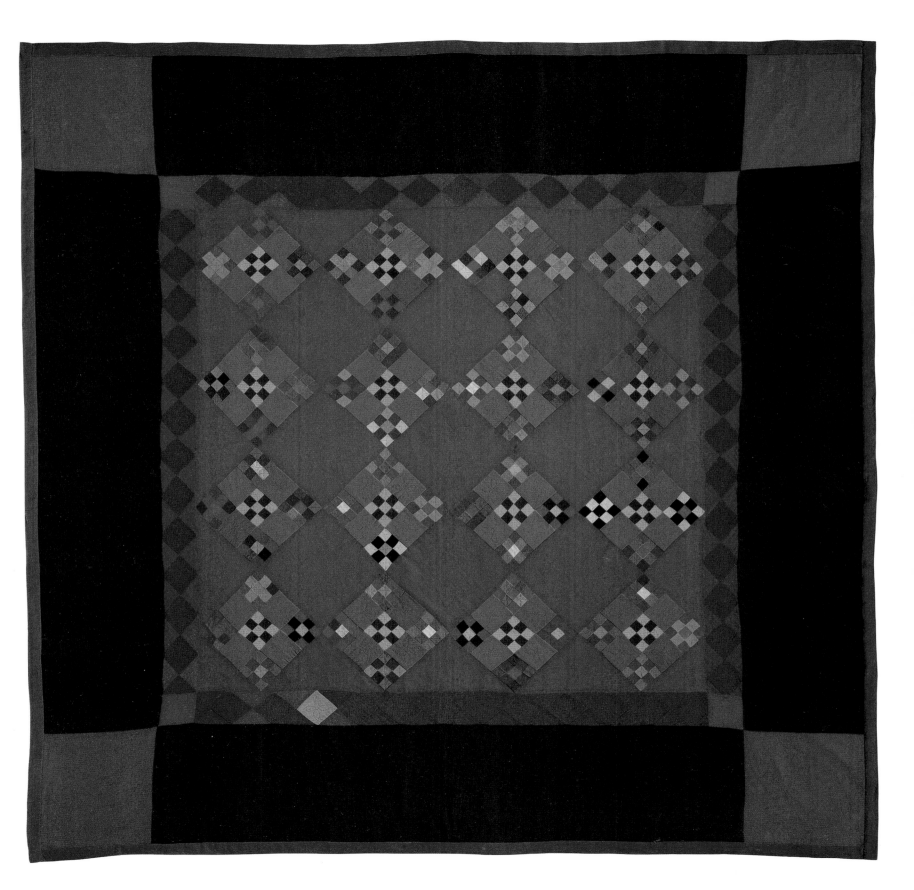

D o u b l e   N i n e p a t c h

*Unknown Amish quiltmaker, American, Lancaster County, Pennsylvania, Circa 1900, Pieced wools, 70 x 82 inches, 585.235*

In Lancaster County, centers of quilts are sometimes "scrappy," but borders and bindings are usually not.
Women sometimes designated the top of their quilts with a border or binding of a different color (see Plate 42).
Embroidered on the back of this quilt are the initials "RE," most likely representing the intended recipient. Quilts were often gifts to friends and family,
celebrating and strengthening the social ties that are so essential to Amish life.

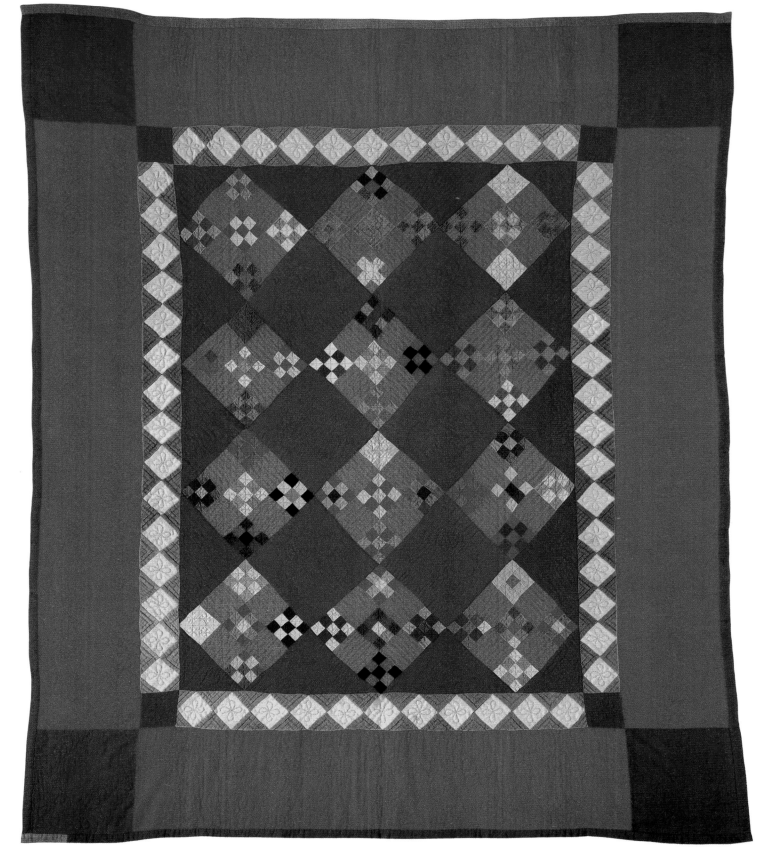

## Double Ninepatch

*Unknown Amish quiltmaker, American, Lancaster County, Pennsylvania, Circa 1920, Pieced wools, 83 x 83 inches, 585.294*

The diamond appears in Lancaster quilts even when it is not the central design element. Amish women regularly stitched it into the narrow inner borders of their quilts; in Double Ninepatch quilts, they pieced the diamond into the frame rather regularly. And when they set their square blocks on point, the motif was echoed yet again.

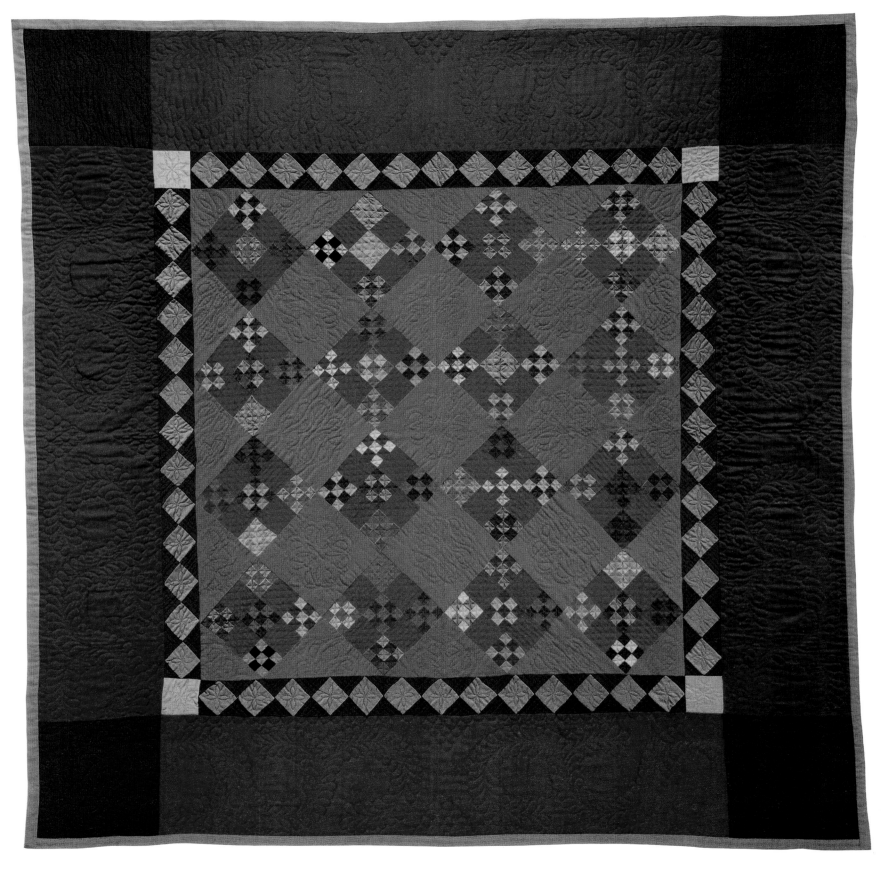

# Double Ninepatch

*Unknown Amish quiltmaker, American, Lancaster County, Pennsylvania, Circa 1930, Pieced wools, 80 x 82 inches, 585.136*

Compare the "set" of this Double Ninepatch to the others in this section (Plates 69–71). Most are set off with plain alternate blocks; this one uses a "grid" to separate the Ninepatches.

Studying Lancaster quilts can require of us something of the discipline and attention to detail that characterized Amish life. We become increasingly observant, noticing small distinctions that might be considered insignificant in a more liberal culture.

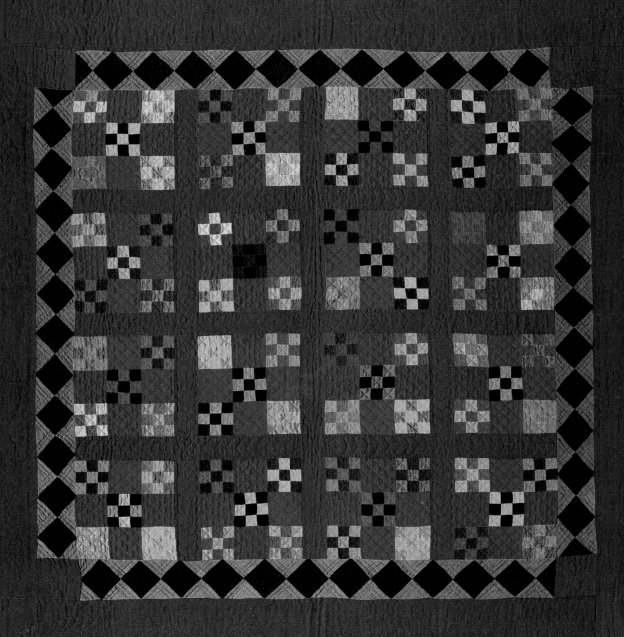

### T r i p l e   I r i s h   C h a i n

*Unknown Amish quiltmaker, American, Lancaster County, Pennsylvania, Circa 1910–20, Pieced wools, 80 x 82 inches, 585.006*

Some patchwork designs, like Irish Chain, were worked by both the Amish and the "English."
Lancaster Amish quilts can be rather easily recognized, though, once you are familiar with their palette, layout, fabrics and quilting.
Amish women purchased factory-produced cloth of rich colors like these by mail, from traveling merchants or from local stores as early as 1850.

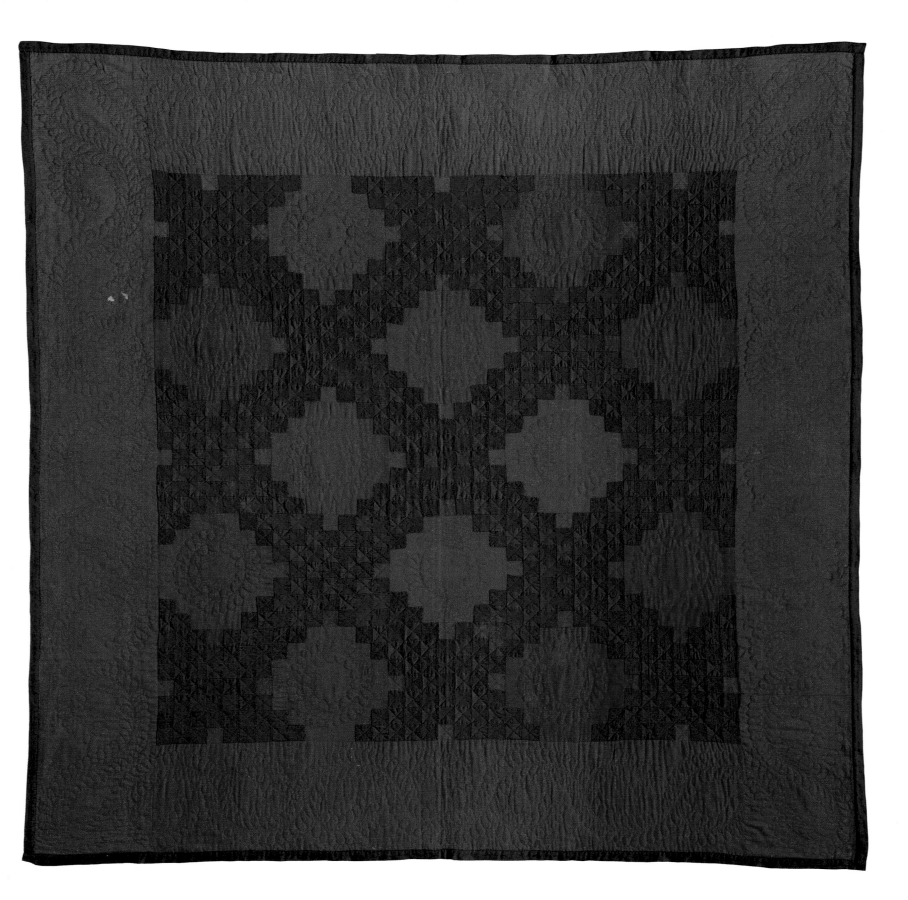

Double Irish Chain

*Unknown Amish quiltmaker, American, Lancaster County, Pennsylvania, Circa 1920, Pieced wools, 70 x 83 inches, 585.215*

The Double Irish Chain design is a simple Twentyfive Patch with a few squares appliquéd to the plain alternate block to complete the diagonal "chain." This and its cousin, illustrated in the previous plate, have the deep, radiant tones and superb quilting that typify Lancaster quilts. Both examples float within a single wide border and are finished with a wide binding, usually of a contrasting color.

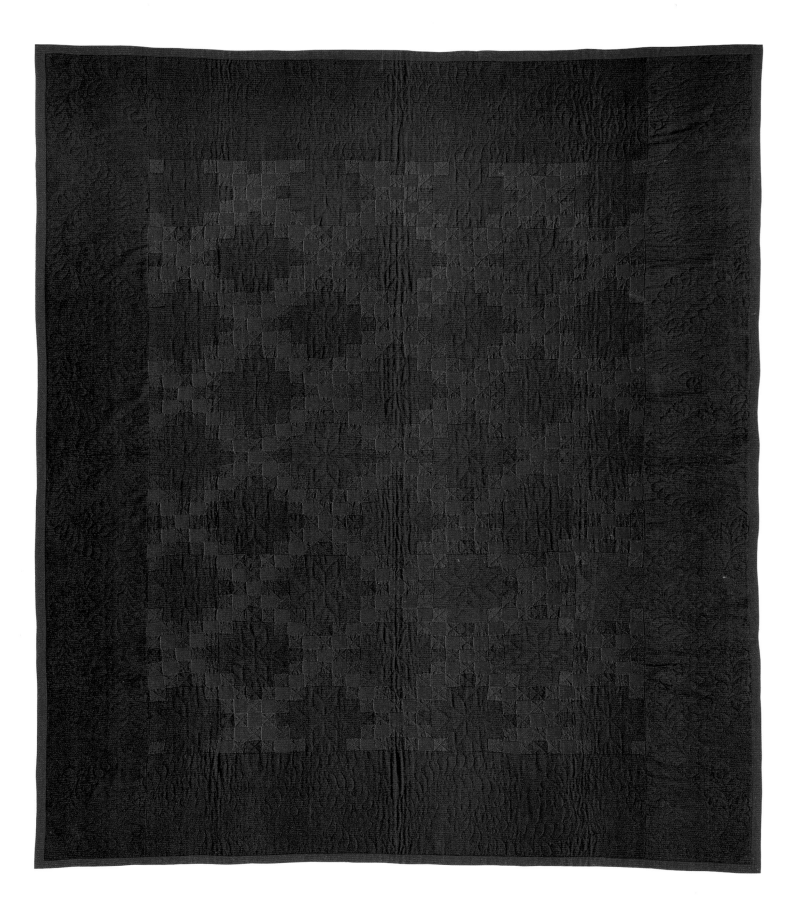

## C o u r t h o u s e   S q u a r e

*Unknown Amish quiltmaker, American, Lancaster County, Pennsylvania, Circa 1910, Pieced wools, 76 x 76 inches, 585.148*

Courthouse Square is another design the Lancaster Amish borrowed, but only rarely, from their neighbors.
Like their "English" counterparts, Amish women at times quilted alone and at other times in groups. With rare exceptions, though, the quilt top
(the surface layer that displays the patchwork design) was designed and pieced by an individual woman.

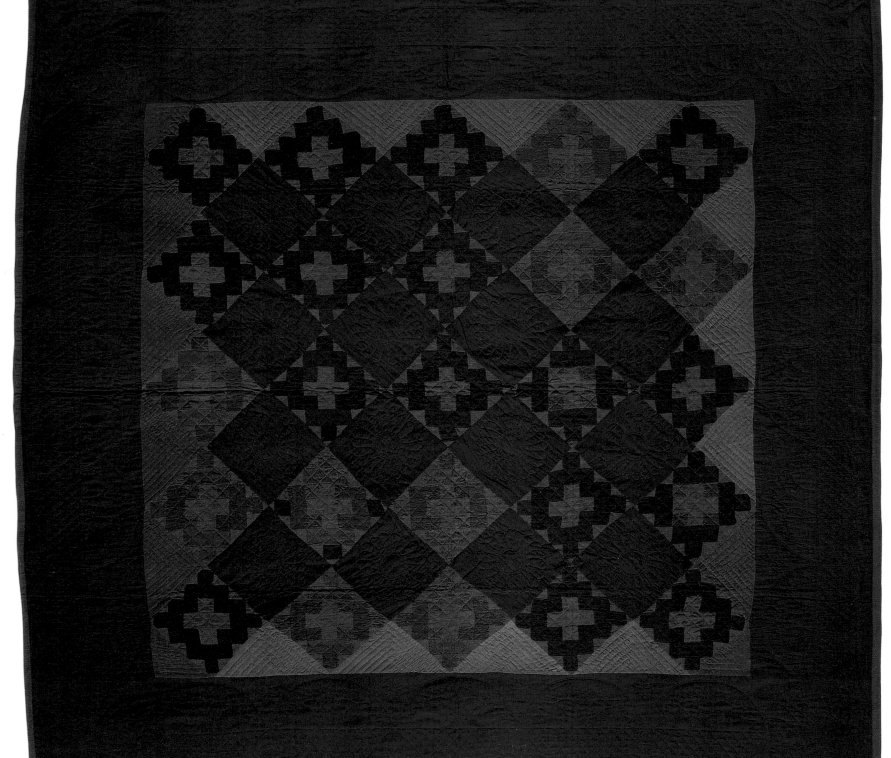

Basket of Chips

*Unknown Amish quiltmaker, American, Lancaster County, Pennsylvania, Circa 1920, Pieced wools and rayons, 76 x 74 inches, 585.247*

Few Lancaster quilts are set together in this way: diagonals are accentuated here by the brilliant red "sashing"
placed around the blocks like diamonds. While the format is something of a departure from convention, the quilt otherwise remains squarely
within the bounds of the Amish aesthetic.

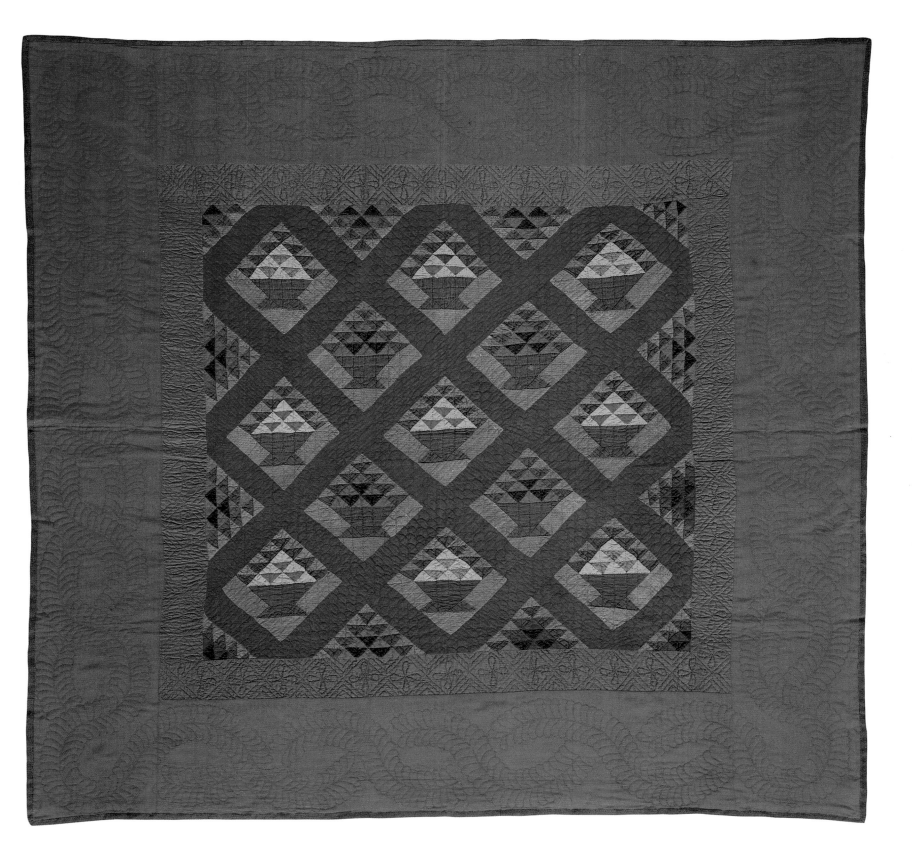

Baskets

*Unknown Amish quiltmaker, American, Lancaster County, Pennsylvania, Circa 1935, Pieced wools, 81 x 81 inches, 585.268*

Baskets, both pieced and quilted, were popular in Lancaster, especially in this century.
This particular piece, though, looks a bit like its Midwestern Amish cousins in its seriality and harsher, more contrasting color mix.
Our source tells us that he knows of four almost identical quilts made in the Smoketown area, where this was collected.

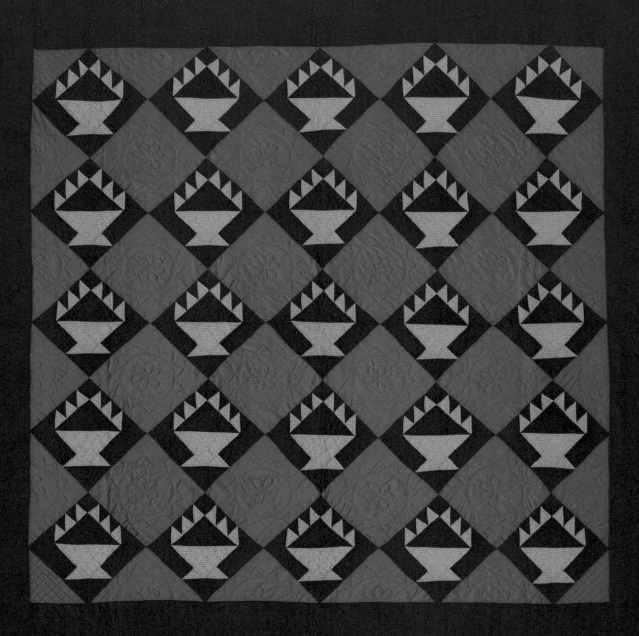

# C r a z y   Q u i l t

*Unknown Amish quiltmaker, American, Lancaster County, Pennsylvania, Circa 1920, Pieced wools, 70 x 80 inches, 585.279*

In pottery, "crazed" glazes crackle into odd and unpredictable shapes. The term "crazy" in patchwork refers to the similarly random-shaped pieces that compose the quilt. In Lancaster, these bits and pieces tend to be organized into contained "crazy" squares relieved by the plain, unpieced blocks and half-blocks set next to them.

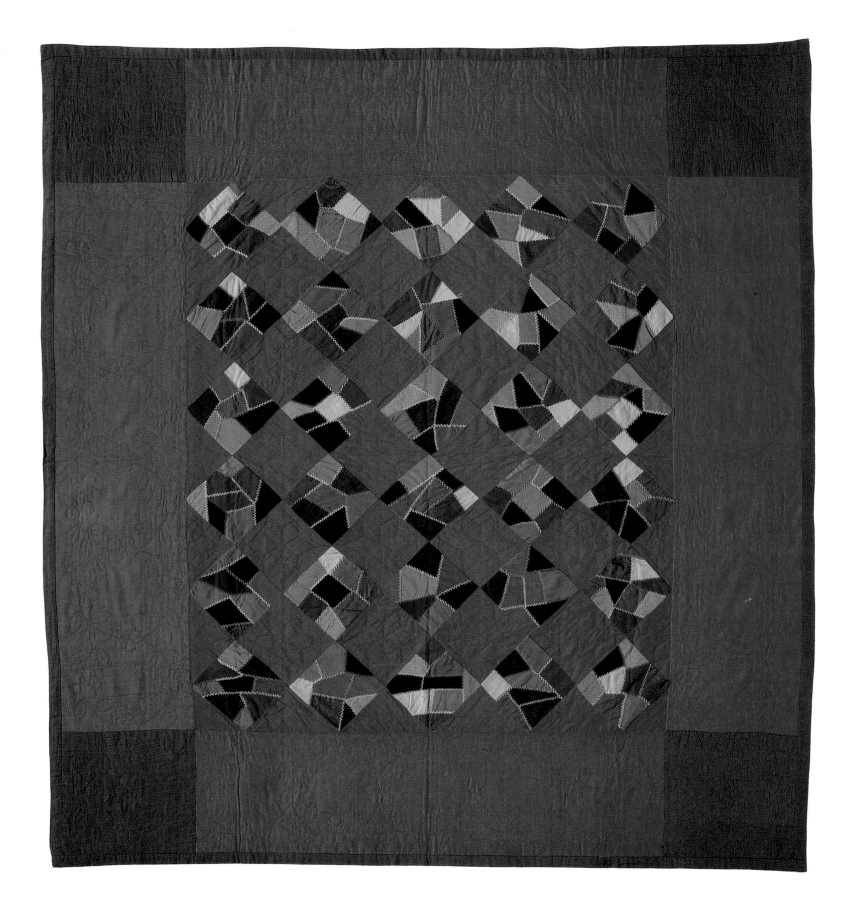

## C r a z y   Q u i l t

*Unknown Amish quiltmaker, American, Lancaster County, Pennsylvania, Dated in embroidery: "1925," Pieced wools, 80 x 80 inches, 585.051*

Some are surprised to find that the Amish made crazy quilts, generally thought of as the most excessive and fussy of American quilts.
It was thirty or forty years after the rage for crazy quilts in the larger culture that Amish women began making them. These twentieth-century Amish
interpretations were quite simple relative to the wildly embellished Victorian examples on which they are modeled.

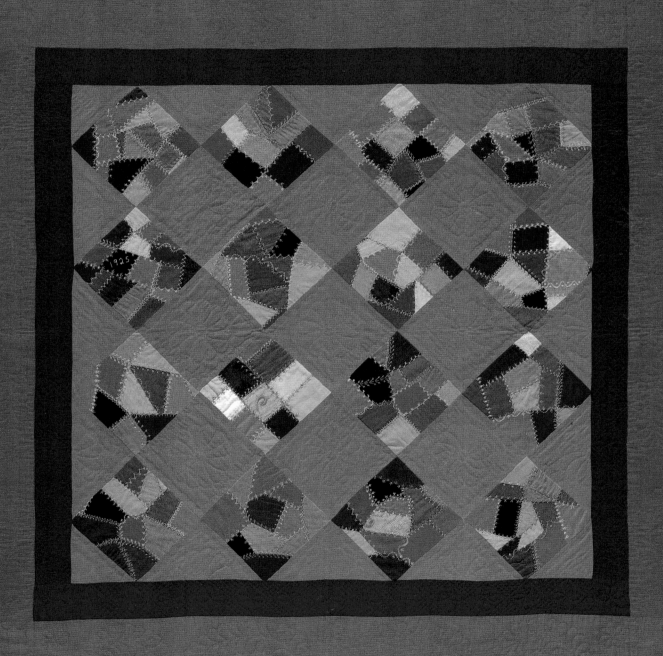

## C r a z y   Q u i l t

*Made by Mrs. Gorman, Amish quiltmaker, American, Lancaster County, Pennsylvania, Circa 1920, Pieced wools, 77 x 92 inches, 585.284*

Our source bought this piece from the maker in the town of Lampeter in Lancaster County. Mrs. Gorman may have displayed a bit of boldness
in choosing to do crazy-quilt blocks, but she also allied herself with her group by placing her blocks in the traditional Lancaster setting and by quilting the
motifs used by the Amish for generations before her.

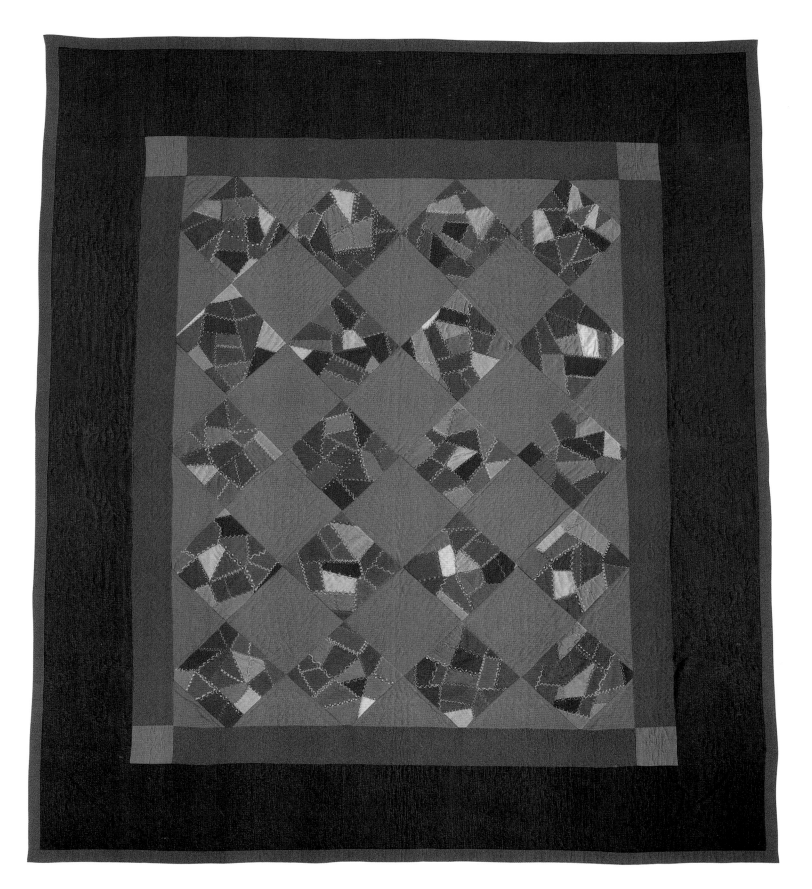

81

## Crazy Quilt

*Unknown Amish quiltmaker, American, Lancaster County, Pennsylvania, Dated in embroidery: "1938," Pieced wools and rayons, 81 x 82 inches, 585.050*

Crazy quilts allow for some significant departures from tradition for Lancaster women. Each block permits a small, free-form composition. Curved seams, virtually never seen in other Lancaster County Amish quilts, can be included. Simple embroidery was also tolerated in crazies, and here, the quiltmaker even used yellow, a color normally considered "showy" in Lancaster.

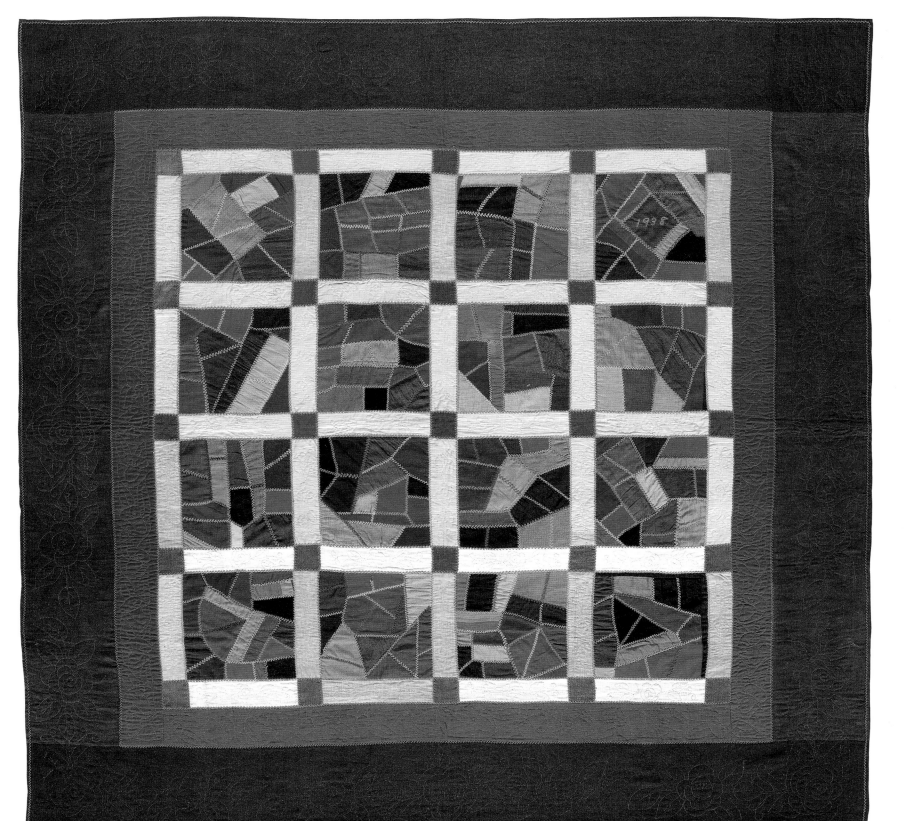

82

## Lone Star

*Unknown Amish quiltmaker, American, Lancaster County, Pennsylvania, Circa 1920, Pieced wools, 88 x 89 inches, 585.001*

The Lone Star, a pattern borrowed from the "English," appears infrequently in Lancaster County Amish quilts. Its strong central motif is compatible with Lancaster sensibilities, but there is often a pulsating, outward energy in the Lone Star that may compromise the usual quiet interior feeling of their quilts. The dynamic movement, achieved by the careful placement of color, is finally contained by the weight of the darker plum border.

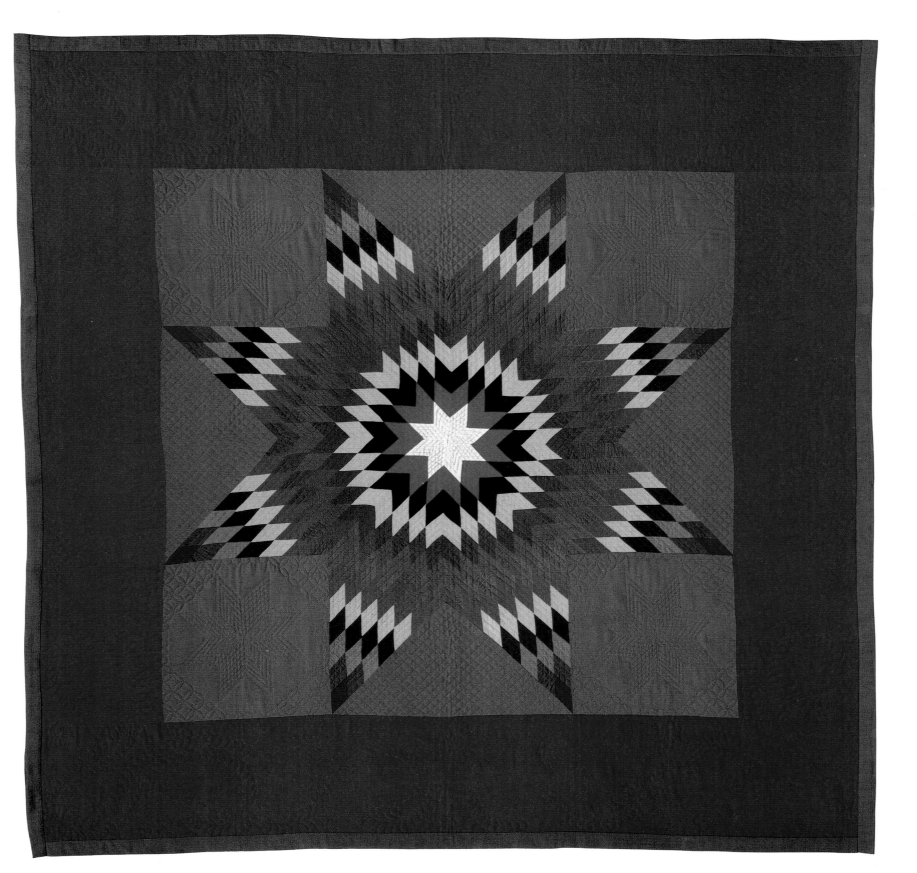

# AFTERWORD

In 1971 Esprit moved into a new building at 900 Minnesota Street in San Francisco. The office areas of this turn-of-the-century brick-and-wood converted winery had high walls that pleaded for some form of decoration. It is difficult to remember when the idea of collecting quilts first took root. But it was directly prompted by the need to put *something* up on those bare walls. Large, colorful and made of textiles, quilts fitted neatly with our business of producing clothing based on good design, color, graphics and workmanship.

At this stage, my personal vision regarding quilt collecting had not been formulated. I set off to local antique shops and quilt dealers to find something suitable and inexpensive. I soon discovered that, as in all things, there is a vast diversity of quilts. I bought a dozen or so traditional quilts from various regions and in a mixture of patterns. I covered the walls of the office, and had discovered quilt collecting.

I began to read about quilts. I hung around quilt shops, went to museums and absorbed all I could on the subject. That same year I went to the East Coast and met Rhea Goodman, a prominent dealer in antique quilts. It was then that I first saw an Amish quilt. I was struck as if by a thunderbolt, bought it and, from that moment on, had eyes only for Amish quilts. This was, quite simply, the turning point that led to the quilt collection as it is now. Though I did add a number of non-Amish patterns during the next few years, the great majority of the additions were of Pennsylvania, Indiana or Ohio Amish origin.

Slowly, but still somewhat recklessly and without enough knowledge or discipline, the collection grew. By 1975 it had reached a respectable level of quality and consisted of about ninety pieces. Soon there were not enough walls, and we were forced to lay many of the quilts in storage. Worried about leaving them unprotected in a bustling office, I kept the most precious pieces at home. Then, early in 1976, a disastrous fire destroyed the main building on Minnesota Street along with ninety percent of the quilts. It was fortunate that the best of the collection was not on the premises, but a number of masterpieces, along with many quite respectable quilts, perished.

The offices were rebuilt during 1976, specifically designed as a "mini-museum" to display the undamaged balance of the collection. We incorporated into the plans proper precautions to take care of our prized quilts. We also decided to open the building to the public and create a self-guided tour of the quilts on display.

With the completion of this new space in 1977, special effort and renewed energy increased both the size and the quality of the collection. The brilliant graphics and contemporary feeling of the Amish quilt that had first sparked my imagination provided the focus for my collecting "eye," and I sold almost all non-Amish and non-Mennonite quilts.

Gradually, through persistence and patience, the collection became known in quilt-collecting circles, and I was soon recognized as a collector capable of making quick decisions and purchasing museum-quality quilts. Opportunities arose, therefore, of which we took advantage, and which enabled us to continue our building and refining process.

The process of narrowing and focusing a collection can be very satisfying after the initial phase of acquisition. Not all collections are submitted to this refinement, which I find unfortunate. As a collector of twentieth-century figurative painting, I have had the opportunity to observe the formation of numerous collections. What I have noticed most particularly is how a defined point of view often decreases as the collection grows. Distractions, boredom, changes in taste and compromise between collecting partners often seem to lead to the fragmentation of the collection's message. I have found in my own collecting a need for tough self-discipline to enable me to adhere to the principle that a collection as a whole should always be greater than the sum of its parts.

One of the biggest factors that can derail this process is cash. In collecting, as in most aspects of life, money has a way of corrupting the soul. It hampers the development of a strong, enduring collection with resolute character and subverts the need for discipline. In short, money does not hone the eye. To counteract this insidious undermining of collecting skills, I have tried to keep a tighter and tougher rein on my acquisitive side, and in 1980, I consciously began to sell pieces that were inferior to new purchases. Today the collection is being whittled down to half its original size, emphasizing quilts of exceptional quality with a strict regional focus: Lancaster County, Pennsylvania, the true origin of this genre of quilts and, for me, the locale where Amish quiltmaking found its richest expression.

This drawdown process is difficult, yet exhilarating. Each acquisition represents a

206 considered choice at the time and enters the collection as a prized newcomer, met with the anticipation that greets a newborn. The quilts are, in effect, one's babies. Throwing them from the nest is tough, but sentiment gives way to the overall goals of the collection. The more selective that one is about the total number of quilts, paintings, sculptures, stamps or whatever in one's collection, the better the chance of accumulating real masterpieces. After all, only so many great pieces exist. Thus one's drive to find them — often the difference between a good and great collector — must be made always stronger.

Today, as I find pleasure in collecting fewer but finer things, I have come to find this refining process a maturation common in growing older. I increasingly take special joy in those material possessions that do not contribute to the present flagrant consumption of resources, and are not new things generating the demand for even more new things. Perhaps it is the influence of the times, my own upbringing, the effects of being for years in a business that caters to consuming and to fashion. But I see more and more people of all ages who realize that discovering, seeing, learning and understanding can be far more rewarding than "having." I am fortunate to be the guardian of these wonderful objects, the reflection of a culture that believes strongly in the virtues of simplicity, unworldliness and denial of material wealth. I hope I have learned at least a little from the people who refined in their art an elegance so simple, yet so rich. For me, this is the real art of the quilt.

Douglas Tompkins

**Acknowledgments**

A project such as *Amish: The Art of the Quilt* represents the work of many people. It is a pleasure to be able too express our gratitude to some of those who contributed. Many thanks to:

Tamotsu Yagi and the Esprit Graphic Design Studio for their work in designing the book. Nicholas Callaway. Natacha Vassilchikov and Caissa Douwes of Callaway Editions, Inc. for their professional guidance. Eve Wheatcroft Granick for sharing her insightful knowledge of Amish women and their quilts and for her book on the subject. *The Amish Quilt*. Barbara Austin. Michael Kile and Susan Rawlins. for their patient and wise editorial counsel. Kathleen Callahan Anderson. Linnea Davis. Sharon Risedorph. Del Rae Roth and David Schump for professional contributions far beyond what was asked. Pat Ferrero. Jonathon Holstein and Kate and Joel Kopp for their helpful comments and suggestions. Tracy Gary for lending perspective and constant support.

Additional thanks to: Kate and Joel Kopp of America Hurrah Antiques. New York: Michael Malce of Kelter-Malce Antiques. New York: Stella Rubin. Potomac. Maryland: and David Wheatcroft of Wheatcroft Antiques. Lewisburg. Pennsylvania.

**Bibliography**

Following is a short list of books on the Amish and their quilts. For a comprehensive bibliography. see Eve Granick's definitive book on the subject. *The Amish Quilt.*

Bishop. Robert. and Elizabeth Safanda. *A Gallery of Amish Quilts*. New York: E.P. Dutton. Inc.. 1976.

Granick. Eve Wheatcroft. *The Amish Quilt*. Intercourse. Pennsylvania: Good Books. Inc.. 1989.

Hostetler. John A.. *Amish Society*. 3rd ed. Baltimore: Johns Hopkins University Press. 1980.

McCauley. Daniel and Kathryn. *Decorative Arts of the Amish of Lancaster County*. Intercourse. Pennsylvania: Good Books. Inc.. 1988.

Pellman. Rachel and Kenneth. *The World of Amish Quilts*. Intercourse. Pennsylvania: Good Books. Inc.. 1984.

Pottinger. David. *Quilts from the Indiana Amish*. New York: E.P. Dutton. Inc.. 1983.

Silber. Julie. *The Esprit Quilt Collection*. San Francisco: Esprit de Corp.. 1985.

**Notes on the Book**

This book has been produced by Callaway Editions. Nicholas Callaway was editorial director. True Sims was production director. assisted by Ivan Wong. Jr.

Editing. layout and sequencing of images were by Douglas Tompkins and Julie Silber. Art Direction. typographic design and layout were by Tamotsu Yagi/Esprit Graphic Design Studio. assisted by Del Rae Roth. David Schump. and Norma Lee.

The typeface for the headlines is Bodoni Antiqua, light and medium. condensed 122 percent. The typefaces for the text are Bodoni Book and Bauer Bodoni. The type was set by Display Lettering + Copy. San Francisco. and Andresen Typographics of San Francisco.

8x10 color photography was made especially for this book by Sharon Risedorph and Lynn Kellner. San Francisco. Whenever possible. transparencies and press proofs were color-corrected by comparison with the quilts.

*Amish: The Art of the Quilt*. second edition. was produced in Hong Kong by Palace Press International. New York. under the direction of Raoul Goff. The illustrations were made from a 175-line screen angled. laser-scanned directly from the previously printed first edition and printed in four-color offset lithography on 128 gms Mitsubishi Matte Art Paper. The cover has been printed in six colors with a matte film lamination. Greg della Stua of Palace Press International coordinated the production services. Gordon Goff was Palace Press International's representative to Callaway Editions.

The book was bound in Hong Kong. The sheets were smyth-sewn in 12 page signatures with the cover drawn-on. The printing and binding of the book was supervised by True Sims. Bruce Andresen and Nicholas Callaway.

First published in the UK by Phaidon Press Limited 1994

Phaidon Press Limited
140 Kensington Church Street, London W8 4BN

Published in association with Callaway Editions, Inc.,
54 Seventh Avenue South, New York, NY 10014, USA

A CIP catalogue record of this book is available from the British Library.

ISBN 0 7148 3136 0

Front Jacket: Diamond in the Square, circa 1920.
Unknown Amish quiltmaker, American, Lancaster County, Pennsylvania.

Pieced Wools, 78 x 78 inches (Plate 8).

Printed and bound in Hong Kong